Death at Snake Hill

Death at Snake Hill

Secrets from a War of 1812 Cemetery

PAUL LITT
RONALD F. WILLIAMSON
JOSEPH W.A. WHITEHORNE

Ontario Heritage Foundation
Local History Series No. 3

Dundurn Press
Toronto & Oxford
1993

Editing: Doris Cowan
Printing and Binding: Gagné Printing Ltd., Louiseville, Quebec, Canada

The writing of this manuscript and the publication of this book were made possible by support from several sources. The publisher wishes to acknowledge the generous assistance and ongoing support of the **Canada Council**, the **Book Publishing Industry Development Program** of the **Department of Communications**, the **Ontario Arts Council**, the **Ontario Publishing Centre** of the **Ministry of Culture, Tourism and Recreation**, and the **Ontario Heritage Foundation**.
    Care has been taken to trace the ownership of copyright material used in the text (including the illustrations). The author and publisher welcome any information enabling them to rectify any reference or credit in subsequent editions.

J. Kirk Howard, Publisher

Canadian Cataloguing in Publication Data

Litt, Paul
    Death at Snake Hill : secrets from a War of 1812 cemetery

Includes index.
ISBN 1-55002-186-9

1. Canada – History – War of 1812 – Antiquities.* 2. United States – History – War of 1812 – Antiquities. 3. Snake Hill Site (Fort Erie, Ont.). 4. Fort Erie (Ont.) – Antiquities. 5. Excavations (Archaeology) – Ontario – Fort Erie. 6. Fort Erie (Fort Erie, Ont.) – Siege, 1814. I. Williamson, R.F. (Ronald F.). II. Whitehorne, Joseph W.A., 1943– . III. Title.

FC3099.F66A38 1993   971.03'4   C93-094131-4
F1059.5.F66L58 1993

Dundurn Press Limited
2181 Queen Street East
Suite 301
Toronto, Canada
M4E 1E5

Dundurn Distribution
73 Lime Walk
Headington, Oxford
England
OX3 7AD

Dundurn Press Limited
736 Cayuga Street
Lewiston, N.Y.
14092-1797
U.S.A.

Whatever makes the past, the distant, or the future, predominate over the present, advances us in the dignity of thinking beings.

– Samuel Johnson

CONTENTS

Foreword   9
Acknowledgements   11
Preface   13

Prologue
BACKHOES, BONES, AND BUREAUCRACY   15

Chapter 1
SYMPATHY AND CURIOSITY   19

Chapter 2
DIGGING INTO THE PAST   41

Chapter 3
THE ARCHIVES AND THE LABORATORY   75

Chapter 4
STEPS TO THE GRAVE   96

Chapter 5
PROOF OF CITIZENSHIP   122

Epilogue
THE SNAKE HILL LEGACY   147

Appendix: Project Team and Researchers   151
Endnotes   153
Index   155

FOREWORD

The Ontario Heritage Foundation Local History Series provides financial assistance for the publication of original works of high quality that offer Ontarians a better understanding of their history. Publications in the series are directed to a broad public audience.

Death at Snake Hill exemplifies the goals of the Local History Series. On one level, this fascinating book is a good detective story. It traces the discovery, excavation, and interpretation of human remains from the War of 1812 that were uncovered in April 1987 at Fort Erie, Ontario. *Death at Snake Hill* is also an illuminating case study, in which heritage concerns can be seen in their broader political and economic context. It also demonstrates the present-day relevance of history and archaeology to our modern society.

I believe that the publication of *Death at Snake Hill*, the third volume in the Foundation's Local History Series, will be welcomed by anyone interested in the history of the land that is known to-day as Ontario.

Dorothy Duncan
Chair
Ontario Heritage Foundation

ACKNOWLEDGEMENTS

The people most responsible for the success of the Snake Hill dig were the archaeologists who worked on the Archaeological Services Inc. team – Andrew Clish, Martin Cooper, Beverly Garner, Robert MacDonald, Julie MacDonald, Deborah Steiss, and Stephen Thomas. We are also grateful to Paul Sledzick and Sean Murphy of the United States National Museum of Health and Medicine, and "honorary archaeologist" Sgt. Jay Llewellyn, a forensic photographer with the United States Army. Equally responsible for the project's achievements were Doug Martin, then deputy mayor of the Town of Fort Erie, Lt. Col. Robert Trotter, formerly with the Army Casualty and Memorial Affairs Operations Centre in Washington, and Susan Pfeiffer, an anthropologist from the University of Guelph who co-ordinated the detailed biological analyses of the remains. In the narrative that follows it was impossible to record all of the important roles that these and other individuals played. We can only acknowledge their contribution at the start and hope the reader will keep in mind the fact that the enterprise described below was a team effort. We are also grateful to Harry Rosettani for adopting a motley crew of archaeologists during its stay in Fort Erie and to Carol Short for her assistance with the preparation of the manuscript.

The Snake Hill enterprise was aided by the support and guidance of the following agencies: the Ontario Heritage Foundation; the Ontario Ministry of Culture and Communications; the Town of Fort Erie; the United States Army; the National Museum of Health and Medicine; the United States Armed Forces Institute of Pathology; the Royal Ontario Museum; the Social Sciences and Humanities Research Council of Canada; the Canadian Armed Forces; Veterans' Affairs Canada; and the Buffalo and Fort Erie Public Bridge Authority.

Finally, the landowners whose properties were invaded and occupied by the Snake Hill dig – Mr. Howard Beattie, Ms. Valerie Beattie, and Mr. Vince Dunn – have our gratitude and respect for their graceful acceptance of unusual circumstances. We hope the rich heritage of their properties will enhance their appreciation of their homes.

PREFACE

The Snake Hill site has been the focus of intensive archaeological investigation and public interest over the past half-decade. With the support of the Archaeological Committee of the Ontario Heritage Foundation, a scientific report on the project was published in 1991 (Susan Pfeiffer and Ronald F. Williamson, editors, *Snake Hill: An Investigation of a Military Cemetery from the War of 1812* [Dundurn, 1991]).

Nevertheless, there remained a need for a more popular book that would provide an accessible account of the enterprise for the general reader and document the intriguing history of the archaeological project itself. The academic study was also restricted by scientific probity from offering the kind of speculative and imaginative interpretation of archaeological data that public interest in the Snake Hill project demanded.

It was hoped that a popular volume which performed these tasks would satisfy widespread curiosity about Snake Hill. At the same time it could attempt to demonstrate the value of archaeology and history to our society. We hope this book will provide a fitting conclusion to the entire Snake Hill enterprise by communicating to the public directly and dramatically the benefits reaped from public investment in such projects.

Paul Litt
Ronald F. Williamson
Joseph W.A. Whitehorne

PROLOGUE

BACKHOES, BONES, AND BUREAUCRACY

It all started with an anonymous call. On 21 April 1987, a man phoned the Niagara Regional Police station in Fort Erie and reported that human skeletons were being unearthed at a building site on Lakeshore Road, just west of Old Fort Erie. The construction workers, he said, were simply shovelling the bones aside as they excavated the basement for the new house they were building.

The police are accustomed to dealing with all kinds of strange tips, some factual, some fanciful. A lakeside home was under construction at the site referred to by the caller. It was one of many new houses being built in an old working-class neighbourhood of former cottages. Was this just some crank who resented the change and was trying to throw a wrench in the works?

An officer was sent to check it out. He arrived at the lot in question, 661 Lakeshore Road, and questioned the construction workers on site. They assured him they had no idea what he was talking about. Since he was acting on an anonymous tip and had no proof, the policeman took them at their word and returned to other duties.

But that wasn't the end of it. The phone rang next in the newsroom of the *St. Catharines Standard*. "I couldn't believe it. The police showed up, asked a few questions and then just left. There's all kinds of bones over there," said the caller, watching the property through his window as he held the receiver. "This has got to be stopped."[1]

The *Standard* dispatched one of its reporters, John Nicol, to check out the story. Nicol walked through the lot and had little trouble finding what looked like a human bone. He took it to the St. Catharines coroner, David Lorensen. The coroner felt that a single bone was hardly enough evidence to warrant taking action, and suggested that Nicol try to retrieve more samples. Beginning to feel he had the makings of a very good story, the *Standard* reporter returned to the site on 24 April to find a backhoe operator filling around the new foundation. The contractor was there as well, and when Nicol claimed to have an amateur interest in collecting old bones, they helped him pick up more than a dozen. "There's at least a couple of bodies in the garage," the contractor told him, explaining that the concrete garage floor had been poured quickly – before word got out.[2]

The reasons for the secrecy were not hard to fathom. Fort Erie is at the foot of Lake Erie where the lake drains into the Niagara River, a natural crossroads of trade since prehistoric times. For native peoples the area had always provided excellent fishing and a source of stone for tools. There have been several Neutral Indian villages in the region within recorded history. As a result, the whole area is littered with ancient bones. Residents unearth them all the time, and have learned that such discoveries bring publicity, red tape, and delays for construction projects. It is better to pretend they aren't there at all. So as spring arrived along Lakeshore Road, the backhoe simply raked through the skeletons. Bones were dumped aside, artifacts pocketed, and skulls smuggled home as curios.

Nicol took his collection to Dr. George Lewis, an anatomist at McMaster University, who told him it contained pieces from at least three different human bodies. Armed with this information, he delivered the macabre hoard to Ontario's chief pathologist in Toronto, who confirmed the bones were human, and also noted that they were very old. On 28 April, the *Standard* published the story. The publicity brought the police back to the scene, accompanied this time by government officials.

There was some confusion about how to proceed. In order to protect the site they needed some means of overriding the lot owners' right to do whatever they wanted with their property. Private property rights came first within the legal system.

The Planning Act had provisions for dealing with archaeological sites. In some development situations an archaeological assessment of the area would have been conducted, which would have resulted in the discovery and exhumation of the burials well before building permits were issued and houses built. But this procedure had not been required in this case. It applied only to new subdivisions, and the Lakeshore Road properties had already existed as cottage lots. As a result, the development was well advanced by the time the bones were discovered. Lot owners had signed a site plan agreement with the municipality, which stipulated that they need only pay for normal services in order to erect houses on their lots. The Town of Fort Erie had committed itself to issuing building permits.

The officials pondered the legal tools at their disposal. Committing an indignity to human remains was a criminal offence, but this law, like the Coroner's Act, had been framed with more recent burials in mind. It seemed that the only applicable legislation was the provincial Cemeteries Act. In the case of the house under construction, the graves had already been desecrated and it was too late to prove that a cemetery had been disturbed. But the Cemeteries Act did provide a way of dealing with any bones that turned up on other lots. It required the owners of properties containing cemeteries to pay for a complex and time-consuming process of moving all graves before they could build on their sites.

Since the Town of Fort Erie had promised the owners that they could build, it felt somewhat responsible for their predicament. Officials from the Heritage Branch of the Ontario Ministry of Culture and Communications (MCC) hinted that the Cemeteries Branch of the Ministry of Consumer and Commercial Relations (MCCR) could order that no further building permits be issued on the vacant lots on Lakeshore Road.[3] Picking up its cue, the town voluntarily withheld further permits. Everyone waited to see what would happen next.

It was a classic confrontation between development and heritage interests. Such conflicts had occurred with increasing frequency during the Ontario land boom of the 1980s. Across the province, developers had been constructing subdivisions, shopping malls and industrial parks at a furious pace. In the process, old neighbourhoods and landmarks were visibly changed, even obliterated. Less obvious were the unprotected and unknown archaeological sites that were ploughed aside by bulldozers working in seemingly vacant fields.

But the rapid development of the 1980s stimulated its own countermovement. Groups concerned about the destruction of environmental, historical, architectural and archaeological sites became more active. They were an unlikely conglomeration of forces, running the gamut from anti-establishment activists to conservative blue-bloods. Articulate and influential, they got the attention of the media and the government. Their message also struck a responsive chord with a general public that was familiar with environmental issues and prepared to weigh development proposals carefully.

The Ontario government had responded to public concern about heritage issues by integrating some protective mechanisms into its applications of the Planning Act and the Environmental Assessment Act. The ramifications were extensive. In the case of archaeology the province needed to employ professional archaeologists to review applications for land development. A new branch of bureaucracy sprang to life. At the same time there was a need for archaeological assessments of development sites. A small private consulting industry was born. The bureaucrats used the consultants as a source of objective expert opinion, and the consultants depended on the bureaucrats to invoke the authority of law. Together they cultivated local contacts and grassroots political support for their work. The increasing prominence of First Nations issues helped the cause. Most of the archaeological sites in Ontario were left by prehistoric peoples and have special cultural and spiritual significance for their descendants. As the 1980s progressed, archaeological issues gained more and more public sympathy and government attention.

In a way it was not really fair that Fort Erie would be the spot where the archaeology lobby would find a *cause célebre.* It was not part of the "Golden Horseshoe," the prosperous region around the west end of Lake Ontario where development pressures were most intense. On the other hand, there were so many archaeological sites in the Fort Erie area that the discovery of another one was not surprising. For years archaeologists had been urging Ontario municipalities to create master plans to determine the archaeological potential of lands before they were zoned for development. Local governments that did so minimized their risk of becoming embroiled in confrontations like the one that had developed on Lakeshore Road. Fort Erie, despite the archaeological wealth within its jurisdiction, had not yet taken this step.

Ignoring the problem had not made it go away. A decade earlier it might have been possible to destroy an archaeological site with no objection from anyone, but by 1987 the rules of the game had changed. An anonymous call had set in motion a process that would uncover one of the most interesting historical archaeological sites in Ontario.

Chapter 1

SYMPATHY AND CURIOSITY

The Town of Fort Erie had a problem. It had approved development on building lots that had turned out to be full of human bones. The provincial government, thinking the Lakeshore Road site might be a cemetery, wanted building permits withheld until the nature and extent of any burials were determined. On the other hand, the lot owners had invested their savings in these properties with the expectation that they would soon be able to build new houses and move in. The town was caught in the middle. So were the bones.

The natural response was to ignore the problem in the hope it would go away. There was no established procedure or familiar precedent to fall back on. As a result, little was done during the months that followed the discovery of the bones in the spring of 1987. But as summer wore on, the lot owners' grumblings intensified. Their discontent was politically troublesome, even more so when the town solicitor advised Mayor Heinz Hummel that they had grounds to sue the municipality. By August the prospect of being liable for hundreds of thousands of dollars in damages stirred the council to action.

It turned to Dr. Ron Williamson, an archaeologist experienced in dealing with both Euro-Canadian and prehistoric native sites in Ontario. Williamson had founded Archaeological Services Inc. (ASI) to provide consulting services required by provincial planning and environmental assessment legislation. Preparing archaeological assessments for lands slated for development was ASI's stock in trade; it had completed dozens since its incorporation in 1980. In this case, the archaeological survey just came a little later than usual.

The owner of one of the Fort Erie lots was particularly anxious to build, and in August 1987 Williamson and his crew arrived to conduct a careful examination of that one lot. This property was about 100 metres west of the house owned by David and Judy George, where the bones had been reported four months earlier. William Fox, a senior archaeologist with the provincial Ministry of Culture and Communications who had visited the site in the spring, showed up to observe the proceedings. The ASI team placed test pits around the lot and discovered that the ground below was a complex layering of organic soils and sandy sedimentary deposits from the lake. After narrowing down the area most likely to be of interest, they rented a Gradall, a piece of heavy machinery well suited to archaeological work. With caterpillar tracks and a shovel mounted on a long telescoping arm, the Gradall could be parked right at the edge of a study area, then reach out to strip soil back without intruding on the site itself. In the hands of an experienced operator it could peel off topsoil cleanly and scrape subsoil away in very thin layers so that the archaeologists would miss nothing underneath. Although there was evidence of prehistoric remains in the vicinity, the ASI team found nothing on the lot itself.

The lots immediately west and east of the George house were still unexamined, but it was October before the town called ASI back to survey them as well. Williamson and his team inspected all the remaining lots west of the George house and found no evidence of any burials. On Monday, 26 October they moved to the property of Vincent Dunn, immediately east of the George house. In the dirt left over from the construction that spring they found part of a human jaw, some teeth, and a piece of arm bone. It was impossible to determine the cultural affiliation of these fragments because they had not been found in an undisturbed state. If they had been, their situation and surroundings might have provided clues to their origins. Williamson feared that the necessary evidence had been obliterated forever by the construction of the house next door. But were there other graves, intact, on the Dunn property?

The answer would come the next day. Once topsoil has been removed, the exact location of a burial is easy for a trained eye to spot because the mixture of topsoil and subsoil used to fill in a grave remains a slightly different colour from the surrounding earth. On Tuesday morning

THE ARCHAEOLOGIST

I n popular culture there is a standard image of archaeology in which the wise old European professor, bespectacled and pith helmeted, orders his men to pry aside the last stone block hiding King Tut's tomb. We tend not to think of archaeology as an activity that can take place in our own backyards. Yet archaeologists are at work on sites that are all around us. To the trained eye, the familiar landscapes of Ontario are full of signs of the peoples who have lived here before. Indeed, many of these archaeological sites are far older than King Tut's tomb.

Ron Williamson got interested in archaeology in 1973. During his first term at the University of Western Ontario, his

Dr. Ron Williamson.

anthropology professor pointed out that there had been human habitation of the surrounding area for about 10,000 years. This fact came as a revelation. Williamson had been taught traditional Canadian history, which emphasized the documented deeds of European immigrants and their descendants. Suddenly his historical consciousness expanded twenty times farther into the past to embrace peoples whose ways of life were all but obliterated by the passage of time. He began to look at the London area in which he had grown up with a fresh perspective and mounting curiosity.

In time this interest developed into a career in archaeology. In the academic world, archaeology is a branch of anthropology, the study of human culture and evolution. The archaeologist discovers the material remains of past societies and interprets their anthropological meaning. To become an archaeologist, Williamson majored in anthropology, completing a B.A. at Western and an M.A. and Ph.D. at McGill University in Montreal. Along the way he acquired a lot of hands-on experience at archaeological digs in the summer months. He worked with people who could tell at a glance if a piece of stone was naturally formed or shaped as a tool by humans, if a bone fragment was from a dog or a raccoon, and a thousand other such significant distinctions. It is from fragments of information such as these that archaeologists piece together the lives of people in the past. Williamson's Ph.D. thesis was concerned with the transition from a hunting-gathering to an agricultural way of life among Iroquoian peoples in southern Ontario between A.D. 800 and A.D. 1250. By the late 1970s he was leading his own archaeological digs to gather information on the subject.

Major changes were under way in Ontario archaeology while Williamson was at university. Before then, universities and museums were about the only employers of professional archaeologists, and the number of practising professionals in Ontario was relatively small. This situation changed in response to mounting public concern about the environmental impact of land development. In 1975, the Ontario government passed the Environmental Assessment Act. It made the approval of major public developments contingent upon impact studies that would assess, among other things, a project's effect upon archaeological sites. The provincial Planning Act of 1979 generated further work in the field by making archaeological surveys a precondition of new subdivision or industrial development.

Suddenly archaeological skills were marketable outside academia. While still a graduate student, Williamson secured a contract from the provincial Ministry of Transportation to study archaeological sites in the area of a highway construction project. Similar jobs followed, and it soon became apparent that he could make a living as an archaeological consultant. The work was interesting and offered more research opportunities than an academic career. In 1980 he founded Archaeological Services Inc. (ASI), operating at first out of his house in London. Similar firms were appearing elsewhere in the province in response to the same demand. As land development accelerated during the 1980s, the fledgling archaeological consulting industry grew apace. By the mid- to late 1980s, consulting archaeology was a milliar-dollar business supporting three or four major firms and a dozen or more individuals working out of their homes or from university labs. ASI now has offices in Toronto and Stratford and is the largest archaeological consulting company in the province.

The work of consulting firms has changed the face of archaeology in Ontario. In the past, archaeologists usually concentrated on sites that were within their areas of specialization. When Williamson was working on his Ph.D., for instance, he only excavated sites that were likely to provide information for his thesis topic. In contract work, however, he never knew what to expect. Often he came across isolated artifacts or sites that were only moderately interesting, but he also made some important finds that otherwise might never have come to light. Development-driven archaeology not only expanded the amount of archaeology being done in Ontario, it increased the frequency of unexpected discoveries of the sort that delight archaeologists and greatly enrich their field of knowledge.

One drawback of contract archaeology is that sites in the path of development cannot always be preserved and excavated at the archaeologists' preferred pace. The very process that leads to their discovery often necessitates their quick removal. This situation is not ideal, but it is better than the alternative – the wholesale destruction of irreplaceable sites that would otherwise take place. Archaeological consultants are conscious of this problem and strive to remain faithful to their profession as well as their clients. They have a responsibility to publish reports of significant excavations to add to the public record of Ontario's past. They have compensated for the time constraints under which they work by improving techniques for recording information about sites. The archaeologists at ASI and other firms, for example, make extensive use of computer technology in their work, developing databases that aid in the recording and analysis of artifacts and settlement patterns.

Contract archaeology often involves close consultation with First Nations groups, who are often clients as well. After all, it was their ancestors who left most of the archaeological sites in Ontario over the past 10,000 years. ASI had worked on a number of native sites around Fort Erie and had also provided expert guidance for the reconstruction of a seventeenth-century Iroquoian village in the area. Through this work and other contracts in the region Williamson became known to officials in Fort Erie. It was natural that they would turn to him in 1987 when they found themselves with an archaeological problem on their hands.

the Gradall set to work on the Dunn lot. Halfway between the street and the lake, and a few feet from the George property line, a rectangular patch became discernible – then another, and another.

The discovery spurred the ASI team into a flurry of excitement and activity. The enchantment of archaeology is most intense at such moments, and archaeologists have to remember to be careful and exacting in an atmosphere of exhilaration and intense curiosity. They chose one promising patch and began trowelling away. The sandy soil was easy to dig through, and they encountered some bones just a few centimetres down. With careful trowel and brush work they revealed the partial outline of a human skeleton, lying face up with its hands folded across its pelvis.

For the site to be considered a cemetery under the Cemeteries Act, there had to be at least one more burial. They moved on to the next patch and performed the same operation. In a few minutes a skull began to emerge from the sandy soil. Below the hollow eyes its jaw, slackened in death, displayed a remarkably white set of teeth that grinned upward as if to greet a long-forgotten sky.

It was a macabre yet fascinating sight. The smiling skull, staring into oblivion, provoked both sympathy and curiosity, making a claim upon the living from the grave. Indeed, the emotions stirred by the newly exposed skeleton reflected fundamental motivations behind the study of archaeology. Onlookers could not help but feel some conflict between these impulses. On the one hand, a sense of identification, a feeling of a common humanity, invoked an instinctive desire to respect the dead and let the skeleton rest in peace. On the other hand, an aura of mystery surrounded the anonymous remains. All kinds of questions sprang to mind. What kind of people had been buried here? How had they died, and why were their graves unmarked?

The questions multiplied as the ASI team located other burials around the lot. At the same time, tentative answers began to emerge. The archaeologists were almost certain they were not dealing with a prehistoric burial ground because of the way in which the skeletons were buried. In prehistoric burials the fetal position was common, and even in those cases where bodies were laid on their backs, the hands were never folded across the pelvis. This was a European custom. The fact that the skeletons' heads were directed west in keeping with Christian practice reinforced the archaeologists' suspicion that they were dealing with historic European burials. Their hunch was soon confirmed. They dusted more earth away from the first skeleton, and below the rib cage and around the spine, they found three little metal discs. Buttons! They had fallen through the body cavity as flesh and clothing had rotted away, and although they were in poor shape after centuries in the soil, their corroded faces still showed definite markings. A stylized "I" was discernible, and they looked like they came from a military uniform. With Old Fort Erie only a few hundred metres away, it seemed likely that the lakeshore properties were situated on a War of 1812 military cemetery. The area had seen major battles between the British and the Americans in 1814, and a bit of checking ascertained that uniform buttons with an "I" had been worn by the American infantry of the day.

With this revelation the discovery took on an intriguing new dimension. The bones by the shore of Lake Erie were a direct link with a critical episode in the history of Canada and the United States. The War of 1812, which had a devastating impact on the Niagara peninsula, had originated far away in the remote realm of European power politics. Britain, desperate for manpower after years of warfare with Napoleonic France, had resorted to stopping U.S. ships on the high seas to search for deserters from the Royal Navy. This high-handed behaviour insulted American national pride and fed the anglophobia of post-revolutionary America. The British were also suspected of inciting unrest among native tribes in an attempt to slow the spread of American settlement into the Ohio valley.

Public resentment of these real or imagined slights gave American politicians popular support for action against their perpetrators. With British military power preoccupied on another continent, a land war in the North American interior offered the tantalizing prospect of easy pickings in Canadian real estate. Although moderate American politicians outnumbered their belligerent colleagues throughout the first decade of the nineteenth century, Congress finally succumbed to the war hawks and declared war on Britain in June of 1812.

In the end the war proved inconclusive, but it remained a historical episode of great significance because of the enduring contribution it made to nationalism on both sides of the border.

The Americans, downplaying their failure to overrun British North America, claimed that the war demonstrated their refusal to submit to British tyranny and completed the revolutionary struggle begun in the 1770s. American public school textbooks referred to the conflict as America's "Second War of Independence."

Canadians had a different perspective. They regarded the Americans as rapacious aggressors who were all too likely to attack again at the earliest opportunity. Canadians became inordinately proud of their success in defending themselves against a vastly superior enemy, and even though the

GRINNER

The second skeleton uncovered at Snake Hill had a full set of teeth and seemed to be smiling jauntily at his discoverers. He quickly earned the nickname of "Grinner" among the project team. Grinner was between twenty-four and twenty-six years old when he died, five feet nine inches (174.1 cm) tall, and a pipe smoker – his teeth were worn from clamping a pipe stem.

Like most of the others, he had been buried with his hands across his stomach. His feet were close together, which suggested that they had been bound before burial. Under the right shoulder blade, there was a fragment of a copper pin which may have been a bandage fastener. This evidence suggested that Grinner may have been hospitalized before his death.

A Buffalo forensic anthropologist, Kathleen O. Arries, became interested in using a skull to reconstruct the facial features and general appearance of one of the soldiers. She chose Grinner because his skull was in better shape than any of the others. Then she began working with a sculptor to rebuild his face. The techniques she employed were those used by police to help identify the skeletal remains of unknown murder victims. Her special expertise was estimating the thickness of tissue that would have covered the bone structure of the skull. The sculptor built up the

Burial 2 as it was revealed.

face with modelling clay according to her instructions. A latex and gauze casting was made, then split off and used as a mould to cast a head in dental stone. Artificial eyes, wigs, and cosmetics were added, creating a likeness similar to a figure in a wax museum. Arries chose to give Grinner blue eyes and reddish brown hair because the American army's records showed that these had been common features among the army's recruits. The wig was cut to a hair style typical of the period. As a result, one of the Snake Hill victims ended up with a face, if not a name.

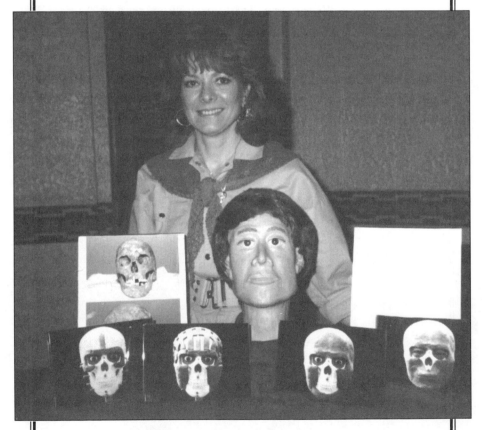

Kathleen Arries and Grinner's image.

British army and allied native tribes deserved most of the credit, the war served as a potent stimulus to a strain of Canadian nationalism distinguished by virulent anti-Americanism.

The newly discovered skeletons provided tangible evidence of this dramatic, half-forgotten conflict. It was not the first time that War of 1812 remains had been found around the old fort. In the early 1930s, a power-shovel excavating a basement for a new house had ripped through three military graves from the war. The story made the newspapers, but no doubt other such incidents had occurred over the years without being reported. During the restoration of Fort Erie in 1938, more skeletons were unearthed, including the mass grave of hundreds of British soldiers killed by an explosion during their attack on American forces at Fort Erie in 1814. These bones were reburied on the grounds with military honours in 1939, and the 2,300 military buttons found with them were conserved and exhibited at the restored fort.

Now history had again reared out of the grave to confront the living. Local residents knew that the Niagara peninsula had a rich military past, but it had rarely revealed itself so dramatically. People began to drop by the excavation site to see the graves, to stare and speculate. Were the soldiers all Americans, or were some of them British regulars or Canadian militia? What part had they played in the conflict, and why had they been buried here?

These were questions that also preoccupied the archaeologists. A full archaeological dig, accompanied by careful historical and scientific research, would be required to find the answers. Williamson believed that such a project was justified. But he had been hired simply to conduct an archaeological survey. Now that he had established the existence of a cemetery of some sort, a decision on what to do next would have to come from the town and the province. In the meantime, the dig was put on hold. The exposed skeletons were covered with tarpaulins and a snowfence erected around the property to keep the curious at a harmless distance. Williamson knew that there were many overly enthusiastic collectors of military artifacts who would not be deterred by a flimsy fence. On

A small American Infantry Script I button found on Burial 1.

his advice, the town also put a security guard on the site twenty-four hours a day.

Once again, officials from the province and the town were perplexed about how to proceed. Legislators had never anticipated a situation of this sort when they framed laws relating to human remains. The Coroner's Act and the Cemeteries Act were not designed to deal with dramatic archaeological finds, and although the Cemeteries Act could be stretched to cover this situation, it was an awkward piece of legislation for the task. It required landowners to add a cemetery designation to their deeds or to pay for the removal and reburial of the bones themselves. In the latter case another regulation specified that no further work could be done on the site for six months while the closing of the cemetery was advertised.

There was also the question of who should or could pay for further work. The Fort Erie town council discussed the problem at a meeting on Monday, 2 November. There was no time for delay. Winter was fast approaching, and its arrival would prevent further digging. It was inadvisable to suspend operations entirely until spring because of the risk of damage to the bones from looting or winter storms blowing in off Lake Erie. But launching a full-scale archaeological dig on the site would be expensive, and no other levels of government had offered any assurances of funding. Nevertheless, the council felt responsible for the landowners' predicament and came up with $10,000 to hire ASI to conduct a five-day archaeological dig. In fact, Williamson and his team had already resumed digging, although until then there had been no guarantee that they would be paid. Town officials had told them that funding would probably be approved, but they were motivated by professional curiosity as well.

It was soon clear that the ASI team had a major discovery on its hands. By Tuesday evening the archaeologists had uncovered four additional graves and evidence of more to come. They had also located pits full of pieces of bone, some of which displayed what looked like saw cuts. It seemed likely that these were limbs that had been sawn off during surgical amputations, which indicated they were near the site of a War of 1812 field hospital.

Word of the discovery was getting around, and public interest continued to mount. Soon crowds of spectators were gathering by the snow fence and journalists from Buffalo and nearby Canadian cities were arriving to observe the proceedings. The ASI archaeologists found themselves constantly button-holed by reporters and peppered with questions from bystanders. The novelty of media stardom quickly wore into exasperation at the constant harassment. Recognizing that it would be more efficient to feed the beast with regular large chunks, Williamson held a press conference at the Fort Erie Town Hall late on Tuesday 3 November. He announced that it was quite likely that at least one of the unearthed skeletons had been an American soldier.

As the importance of the find became clearer, members of the Fort Erie council began to feel a bit overwhelmed about what they had got themselves into. "Our costs are getting to the point where we feel we can no longer afford to do this alone," warned Mayor Hummel on 6 November.[1] The only ray of hope came from across the Niagara River. In pursuit of the story the media themselves had become actors in the drama. Journalists had contacted the United States Embassy in Ottawa to solicit the American response to the discovery. The Americans had not yet been informed through official channels, but they were interested and had passed the news on to Washington. Now a spokesman for the U.S. Army was reported to have said that any remains that were identified as American would be repatriated for burial in a national military cemetery. Perhaps Fort Erie would not have to foot the whole bill for the dig after all.

By the end of the week, Williamson and his crew had found a dozen skeletons without reaching the end of the cemetery. Far from ridding the town of its problem, the five-day dig had only compounded it. Work was suspended again until the funding problem was resolved. In the meantime, news of the discovery spread farther afield. Historians and archaeologists from both sides of the border were calling Williamson with questions, and making arrangements to visit the site. Speculation about the origins of the skeletons filled newspaper columns and television broadcasts, and everyone on the streets of Fort Erie became a historian with a theory.

Some facts were clear. The history books confirmed that there had been American troops in the area. In fact, some of the bloodiest battles of the war had been at Fort Erie after the American army had invaded and captured it in the summer of 1814.

The second American invasion of Fort Erie came more than 173 years later. On Tuesday, 10 November, Williamson and Deborah Steiss of ASI were summoned to the mayor's office, where they were ushered into the presence of three officers of the U.S. Army. Resplendent in full uniform, medals gleaming, Lt. Col. Robert Trotter leaned back in the mayor's chair, his feet propped up on the desk. He was flanked by Major Michael Wood, public affairs officer of the Total Army Personnel Agency, and Lt. Col. Joseph Whitehorne, a historian attached to the Secretary of the Army. Trotter himself represented the U.S. Army Mortuary Affairs Department, which was responsible for the repatriation of the bodies of U.S. soldiers who died abroad. They were an imposing trio, but they turned out to be an affable bunch; most important, they were eager to support and expedite the dig.

Indeed, in their eagerness to arrive at the scene the Americans had overlooked a few niceties of international protocol by neglecting to inform the Canadian government of their intentions. When uniformed soldiers from a foreign army cross an international border, it is considered a hostile act – at least in diplomatic circles. For the moment, however, these Americans had made it into Canada unopposed. Their mission was straightforward: they had come to bring their boys home. Wood told reporters that if the remains proved to be American "they will be rendered the honours due to a member of the armed forces ... fallen in battle."[2] This commitment was an important tradition, a mainstay of army morale and *esprit de corps.*

"We take care of our own," Trotter explained. "We never forget our soldiers. We will bring them home."

"That's what any soldier dreams of – coming home," added Wood.[3] In recent years this mandate had usually meant bringing back the remains of U.S. soldiers from Vietnam. The geographical proximity and temporal remoteness of the Fort Erie discovery provided an interesting diversion from their regular line of work. If the site turned out to be what it seemed to be, it would be one of the oldest unknown U.S. military cemeteries ever discovered. It offered a unique opportunity to learn more about the army's history and to celebrate its glorious past.

With the help of Tim Shaughnessy, the superintendent of Old Fort Erie, the archaeologists had already established the significance of the graveyard's location. The officer responsible for constructing the defensive works at Fort Erie during the American occupation in 1814, a Major Douglass of the U.S. Army Corps of Engineers, had left records that included a detailed map of American fortifications. The Americans had built a defensive line west of the fort and then south to the lake, and the map showed that the burial site was directly outside an artillery battery that had anchored its southernmost tip. The strongpoint, commanded by a Captain Towson, had been located on Snake Hill, a slight rise by the lake a few yards east of where the graves were discovered. The British had mounted a full-scale assault on the Towson battery as part of a bloody and unsuccessful night attack on 15 August 1814. Had Williamson and his crew unearthed the remains of American casualties from that battle?

It would take more historical research, along with painstaking archaeological work and scientific analysis of the bones, to know for sure. Trotter, it turned out, had already begun assembling a team of American specialists who were about to descend on the site. Williamson tactfully, but very firmly, vetoed this plan. The Americans, he pointed out, were in a foreign country where archaeologists had to be licensed in accordance with provincial regulations. Besides, he was there first and it was *his* dig. But he was willing to talk.

They met for dinner that night, and Trotter made a generous offer. He told Williamson that if he needed anything that would help with the dig over the next few weeks – research, logistical support, special equipment, whatever – he had only to ask and the American army would supply it if it could. For an archaeologist accustomed to working with tight budgets and skimpy resources, this was a dream come true. As the Americans became sensitive to the fact that they were in a foreign, sovereign country, the relationship showed promise.

Williamson was grateful for American interest in the project and told them he would happily employ American expertise wherever it was needed. He needed a diverse collection of scholars from the arts and sciences who could bring a variety of perspectives to bear on the puzzle presented by the skeletons. Eventually he assembled a multidisciplinary team composed of experts from both Canada and the United States. Besides archaeologists, there would be historians, anthropologists, conservationists, technicians and an array of scientific specialists from Canada's National Museum of Civilization, the Smithsonian Institution in Washington, the Royal Ontario Museum in Toronto, and a variety of other museums, universities and government agencies.

The collaborative effort to find out more about the bodies promised significant advances in all the disciplines involved. It was not usually possible to check scientific conclusions about archaeological discoveries against other sources of information. But in this case it already seemed likely that at least some of the remains were from American soldiers from the War of 1812. If so, archaeologists and scientists would be able to compare their techniques and conclusions to historical sources. "It was an archaeologist's dream," Williamson later told a magazine interviewer. "We usually have to say something like, the site is from 1800 B.C., plus or minus 300 years. But with this site, we were pleased ... to be able to narrow it down to the year, even the month."[4]

Williamson's immediate concern was to ensure that remains already uncovered were protected from the elements. On 12 November he phoned the Canadian army to see if it could supply some tents. The Central Region Operations Detachment, based in Downsview, Ontario, told him that something could be done in a week or so. When he heard about this, Lieutenant Colonel Trotter was unimpressed. The American army, he said, could deliver tents by four that afternoon. Williamson let the Canadian army know that he had a better offer, and they responded with a promise of tents the next day. In the end, the Lincoln and Welland

BURIAL 1

The first skeleton found was that of a young man between twenty-two and twenty-four years old, about five feet seven inches (170.9 cm) tall, who had been shot through the head. The carbon and nitrogen isotope values for his bones suggested that he was an American from a northeastern state who had eaten a lot of corn and fish, the basic diet of aboriginal peoples at the time.

The holes in this soldier's skull showed that he had been hit in the back of the head by a shot that had continued on and exited through the front of his skull. This was not the first head wound he had suffered (although it probably was the last). On the right side of his head, close to where the shot came out of his skull, there was an indentation caused by a previous injury. His hipbones and his upper thighbones were also badly fragmented. These breaks suggested that his head wound was just one of many injuries that could have resulted from an explosion, or from debris kicked up by the impact of a cannon ball.

The corpse had been laid out on its back in the grave, with its head facing west, its right hand in its lap and its left arm lying alongside its body. The right arm bones had been disturbed, the pelvic bone was missing, and a toe bone was discovered near the hip, which suggested that rats might have disturbed the body after burial.

The twenty-three buttons found around this skeleton were so badly corroded that their markings were no longer discernible. Their distribution in the grave suggested that the soldier had been buried in an American army coatee (short jacket) and overalls. The number of buttons missing and replaced suggested that the coatee and its wearer had suffered some hard use.

A six-centimetre rib fragment from another individual was also found in the grave. It was neatly cut at one end except for a tag of bone which showed that it had been snapped off. According to most medical field records, the chest cavity was seldom opened by military surgeons. If so, this piece of bone was a clue to a rare instance of chest surgery. Since the body that the rib fragment came from was not found at Snake Hill, the patient may have survived at least long enough to avoid burial on Canadian soil.

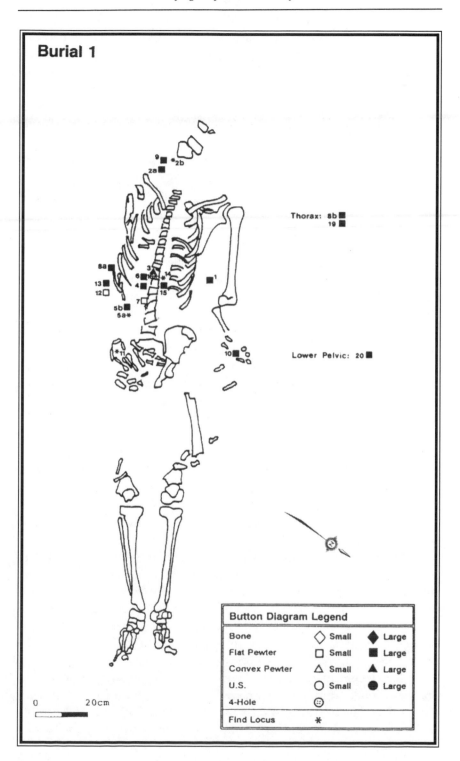

Burial 1

Thorax: 8b
19

Lower Pelvic: 20

Button Diagram Legend

	Small	Large
Bone	◇ Small	◆ Large
Flat Pewter	☐ Small	■ Large
Convex Pewter	△ Small	▲ Large
U.S.	○ Small	● Large
4-Hole	☺	
Find Locus	✳	

0   20cm

Regiment of St. Catharines, Ontario, arrived to erect modular tentage that weekend. A little time was lost, but if the Americans had supplied tents it would almost certainly have created an international incident. The only way that Trotter could have delivered them the same afternoon was to have them flown in by army helicopter, a violation of Canadian airspace that would have compounded the American army's earlier infiltration by land.

With the archaeologists idle, property owners worrying, reporters snooping, spectators gawking, U.S. Army officers parading about, local politicians agitated, and bureaucrats scrambling for answers, the Snake Hill dig was turning into quite a circus. The problem of who would foot the bill for further work was still holding things up. Mayor Hummel contended that Fort Erie simply could not afford any further expenditures, and no other government agencies had yet offered to help. Somehow the mess had to be sorted out. A meeting was organized between all interested parties for the last weekday of the second week of November – Friday the thirteenth.

The gathering brought together all the critical issues and interests involved in the Snake Hill dig. In addition to the town council and some top municipal officials, Williamson, his executive assistant Rob MacDonald, and the property owners were in attendance. The Niagara Region was represented by its chief coroner, Dr. B. Penton. From the province, there was Marie Fitzgerald of the Cemeteries Branch of the Ministry of Consumer and Commercial Relations, William Fox from the Heritage Branch of the Ministry of Culture and Communications, and the area's MPP (member of provincial parliament), Ron Haggerty. Bruce Robertson, an official from Veterans Affairs who had arrived in Fort Erie the day before, and the local MP, Girve Fretz, provided a federal presence. Finally, Lieutenant Colonel Trotter and Major Wood were there on behalf of the American army.

The mayor, selected aldermen, and key employees had met before to plan how to orchestrate proceedings. Their main objectives were to get some estimate of the costs involved if the dig went ahead, to get commitments from higher levels of government to fund the enterprise, and to achieve some consensus about how the dig would proceed when funding became available. To this end, town solicitor Stuart Ellis had prepared a draft of an agreement that they hoped to get everyone involved to sign.

Ellis's document elaborated upon tentative conclusions reached the previous Monday during a meeting in Toronto between town and provincial officials. The consensus was that the Cemeteries Act and the Anatomy Act could be used in tandem to improvise a legal structure for further work. Since the Cemeteries Act applied only to the removal and reburial of the bones, the Anatomy Act would have to be invoked to make legal provision for the time necessary to examine them. ASI could then take the bones to a research site where they could be kept for a period of up to six months. Although these remains did not really qualify as bodies under the Anatomy Act, it was the only legislation available that provided for an interlude for scientific study. When their nationality was ascertained, any American remains would be handed over to U.S. authorities. Canadian or British remains would be the responsibility of Veterans' Affairs, and the town would assume the landowners' responsibility, under the Cemeteries Act, for burying any civilian remains that were found.

This elaborate plan was cobbled together to provide some semblance of legality to the project and to comfort those who felt uneasy operating outside of established legislation. But it was really common sense that dictated how things should proceed. The Ontario government cut through some of the red tape by promising to issue an order-in-council that would waive the provision of the Cemeteries Act that called for advertising the closure of a cemetery for six months. The dig would thus be able to proceed immediately, making it possible for the landowners to build on their lots early the next spring. There was general agreement with this plan, but on other points things began to bog down.

The question of disposition of artifacts discovered on the site generated some acrimony. The Ontario Heritage Act set out licensing terms for archaeologists, which required Williamson to consult with landowners and the ministry about the dispersal of artifacts. Ellis thought that the town should get the artifacts. After all, it was footing the bill; the province so far had paid nothing. But William Fox, the Ontario government archaeologist, was annoyed to hear the province vilified, since he believed it was the level of government most concerned with the need to protect archaeological sites. "This whole situation would have been taken care of through planning if the normal development due process [had occurred]," he said. If plans for the lakeshore site had been properly reviewed by provincial officials, the tell-tale historical and environmental signs would have been recognized and an archaeological survey of the area would then have been ordered. This would have involved some delay in selling the lots affected, but it would have been better than passing the problem on to unsuspecting landowners and creating the current imbroglio.

Town officials did not like Fox's implication that they were to blame for the problem. Ellis, the town solicitor, pointed out that the land had not been subject to the Planning Act. The fact that it had had cottages built on it before meant that it did not qualify as a new subdivision. He went on to say that the Cemeteries Act only affected the property owners; it did not really require the town to do anything. The town had assumed responsibility for the landowners' predicament without any legal obligation to do so. It did not like being accused of wrongdoing when it thought it was going out of its way to be helpful.

Vincent Dunn, the landowner on whose property the bones were lying, interrupted these recriminations with a passionate speech urging that the speedy exhumation of the skeletons and their proper reburial should be the guiding principle for all involved.

His neighbours the Georges were not quite so magnanimous. Mrs. George was afraid that she and her husband would be charged $350 for the legal costs of preparing the agreement under discussion. "That's money we could put towards window frames," she pointed out, and went on to complain about spectators overrunning her property and leaving "nose prints on my windows."[5] She demanded that the town erect fencing around her lot. Her husband had something to add. Mr. George wanted nothing to do with the dig, but he was concerned that somebody might have plans to excavate his property. Everyone at the table had a good idea of what might be found on the George's land, but the consensus was that there was no legal way to force such an extension of the dig against his wishes. It was suggested that for his own peace of mind, and to avoid trouble with the Cemeteries Act in the event of resale, he might voluntarily invite the archaeologists to include his property in their operations. But Mr. George made it clear that he was not likely to do that.

The meeting went on to address the fundamental question of money. Ellis wanted an estimate of costs so that government officials could go to their ministries and get commitments over the weekend. With winter closing in, there was no time to wait for grant applications to be processed in their usual leisurely fashion. The town would expect to hear their responses when it met the next Monday to decide if it would continue to sponsor the dig. Williamson was asked to provide a rough estimate of the expenses that lay ahead. A lot of figures were bandied about, and the total cost for the dig, lab work, and reporting was eventually calculated at $170,000.[6]

The town wanted the federal government to promise to pay at least half of this amount, but it was difficult to pin responsibility for the project on any one federal agency. The Canadian Parks Service made no promises: it was in charge of many similar historic sites, but Fort Erie was the responsibility of the Niagara Parks Commission. Although Veterans Affairs was not responsible for soldiers from pre-Confederation times, Bruce Robertson said that his department would probably pay the costs of burial for any British or Canadian bodies that were discovered. This was not terribly helpful. So far none of the burials had been identified as British or Canadian, and in any case, the costs involved in their exhumation would be far greater than those associated with mere reburial. Once again, the difficulty lay in the unprecedented nature of the discovery. No one had predicted this sort of thing. The funding criteria of established programs were quite specific and did not apply. MP Girve Fretz promised to do what he could in Ottawa to break this impasse and find funding somewhere, even if it meant going through the Prime Minister's Office.

Marie Fitzgerald had contacted the Commonwealth War Graves Commission and reported that the British government did not repatriate remains of British soldiers. The British remembered the legions of their former empire with a fondness that was insufficient to justify the bureaucratic nightmare of bringing home their remains.

On the provincial level things were a little better. William Fox of the Heritage Branch said that although there were no ready funds for such a purpose in Culture and Communications, there was a good chance that special arrangements could be made. MPP Ray Haggerty had been in touch with Fox's ministry and confirmed that the minister might be able to make special funds available.

It would be easy to ridicule all this bureaucratic evasiveness, but in fact the legal and political problems were real. There was no lack of interest or good will, but no single agency had the mandate or authority to promise funding. It was a Catch-22 situation: no one was willing to make a financial commitment until the origins of the bones were known, but the origins of the bones could not be determined unless someone came up with some money. As a result, cautious bureaucrats with tight budgets played a waiting game, hoping that media pressure would force the other guys to move first, or that the Americans would offer to pay the whole shot.

The latter seemed a possibility. The American army gave the firmest commitment about funding to be heard that day. Lieutenant Colonel Trotter emphasized that they wanted the dig to proceed as quickly as possible, and that they would pay their fair share. How much that would be was impossible to say, but he hinted that it would not be simply a percentage tied to the number of American bodies that turned up. This commitment on the part of the American army made a critical difference. The Americans were prepared to honour their war dead and were willing to pay for the privilege. It was a position that piqued Canadian national pride, challenging the provincial and federal governments to show at least an equal concern for a heritage site on their territory and to cough up a fair portion of the costs.

The U.S. Army's pledge became the critical factor that drove the whole project. From this point on it would be the American army's interest in repatriating its soldiers rather than the town of Fort Erie's sense of responsibility that would propel events. Things would have been very different if the bones had turned out to be the remains of natives, unknown civilians, or even British or Canadian soldiers. The American army had to have proof that the remains were those of American soldiers before they could be repatriated. The need to identify nationality justified a full-scale archaeological dig, extensive historical research, and exacting scientific analysis of the bones. In this way a traditional point of American military pride justified a collaborative scholarly project with extensive implications of its own.

All of this process was set in motion by the skeletons that emerged from the sandy soil of the lot on Lakeshore Road. Indeed, the political machinations generated by the Snake Hill discovery were simply more elaborate manifestations of the sympathy and curiosity aroused by the initial discovery. The American army's tradition of repatriating its fallen soldiers was a military embellishment of the universal custom of respect for the dead, while scholarly interest in the discovery was simply a refinement of basic human curiosity about the skeletons. In the case of Snake Hill, the need to identify the nationality of the skeletons made these two impulses entirely complementary. The Snake Hill skeletons would be picked up, dusted off, and escorted home with a soldier on one arm and a scholar on the other.

Chapter 2

DIGGING INTO THE PAST

U p the road from the cemetery stood Old Fort Erie, the War of 1812 stronghold that had brought the Snake Hill victims and countless other soldiers to these shores to die. One of a series of British bastions along the Great Lakes, it was designed to control access to the Niagara River. The British had built a succession of forts on this strategic site following their conquest of New France during the Seven Years' War. The latest was started in 1805, but work had progressed slowly. When war broke out in 1812 the fort consisted of just two barracks flanked by stone bastions and fronted by an earthen parapet on the lake side. A stockade and a ditch were quickly added to protect the inland approach, but there were neither the resources nor the time to do a proper job. Thousands of British and American soldiers would fight over these makeshift walls, and in the end the entire complex would be blown to bits by a retreating American army.

The fort had remained an overgrown ruin for more than a century. In the late 1930s it was restored as a Depression make-work project. The Niagara Parks Commission had run it as a historic site and tourist attraction ever since. Now it was helping to memorialize its victims in another way by housing an office and field laboratory for ASI in its reception building. A phone line linked these temporary facilities to the archaeological

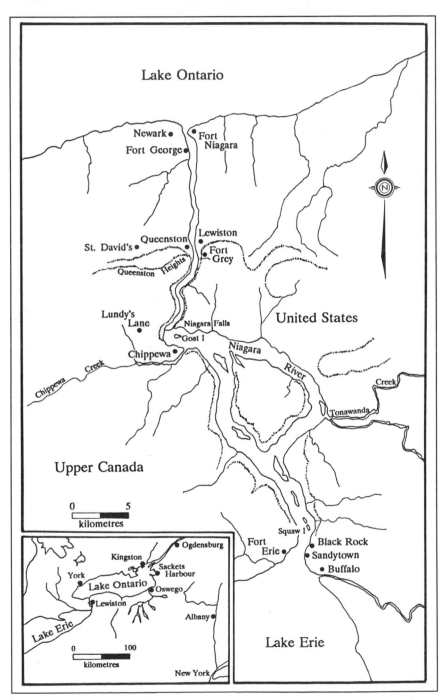

The Niagara frontier: Fort Erie is strategically located in the south, at the mouth of the Niagara River.

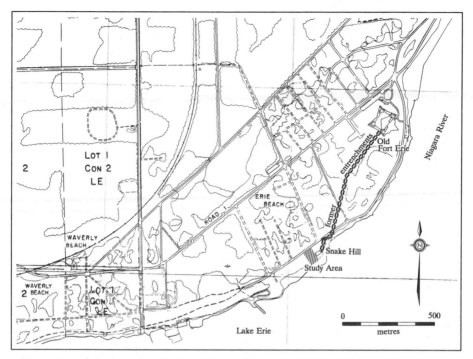

Location of study area – Snake Hill in relation to Old Fort Erie and the streets of the modern town of Fort Erie.

site, re-establishing a connection between the two locations that had been linked by American defensive lines 173 years before.

Down by Snake Hill the dig was in full swing. The barren, windswept lot of a week before was now a well-equipped encampment. A trailer served as an on-site office, and tents protected each burial area from the elements. Under the canvas, electric lights and propane heaters supplied by the town blasted away at the dull and damp November air. Not the least of the new amenities was the baby-blue portable toilet that had been set up near the trailer. Along the snow fence by the road was another fixture – the crowd that gathered day after day to watch all of the strange goings-on.

Other than the odd glimpse of a skeleton, what they saw was a bunch of people in ski jackets and work boots absorbed in a variety of inexplicable activities. They could tell Williamson and his crew of archaeologists from the rest by the blue ASI caps they wore. Otherwise it was possible to confuse a backhoe operator from the township with a scientist from the Smithsonian. Everyone said that there were physical anthropologists on the site, but no one was quite sure what they looked like. The American army officers were easy to distinguish because of their uniforms, but one of them was a historian, and there was an United States Air Force sergeant who was a photographer. It was all very confusing, and there was plenty of gossip to confuse things further.

Some of the archaeologists were busy mapping the location of all the archaeological features discovered to date. East of the first two burials there were a dozen graves in two uneven rows running perpendicular to the lakeshore. Farther east, in the middle of the Dunn property, they had uncovered a septic tank system from a former cottage, which provided a fragrant reminder of a more recent human presence. For the next fifteen metres there was not even a trace of a burial. At first the archaeologists had thought that graves in this area had been obliterated by cottage building years before, but then another skeleton and two medical waste pits had turned up at the east side of the lot. Ten more graves had been found across the property line on the lot of Dunn's neighbours, Howard and Valerie Beattie. Beyond that there was nothing. They decided that this was the eastern limit of the cemetery, but its opposite boundary remained indeterminable. The empty lots to the west contained no burials, and since they had neither permission nor authority to dig on the George property, the exact western limit of the cemetery would never be known. The part they were left with encompassed an area about fifty metres long and twenty-three metres wide, running parallel to the shoreline.

Ruins of Old Fort Erie, 1900.

From *The Pictorial Field-Book of the War of 1812* by Benson J. Lossing (New York: Harper & Brothers, 1868).

The curious onlookers at the snow fence could not see all of the research being conducted by the archaeologists. During the first few days of the dig they spent hours finding out all they could about the War of 1812 and events at Fort Erie in 1814. Fort Erie's superintendent, Tim Shaughnessy, and a local historian, David Owen, were generous in sharing their knowledge of the area's rich military history. Williamson had recruited Lieutenant Colonel Whitehorne as the project's historian, and he began reading all the available secondary sources and planning archival research in American military records. In the meantime the archaeologists themselves cracked the history books to develop a first-hand acquaintance with the background of the bones they were exhuming.

The first thing they learned was that an understanding of the general course of the war was necessary in order to appreciate the campaign of

Mapping of burials.

1814. The American army was a mess – rusty, under-manned, and led by second-rate relics of the Revolutionary era thirty-five years before. The U.S. politicians who declared war had not worried about military preparedness because they foresaw an easy campaign of liberation rather than a difficult war of conquest. Upper Canada, and particularly the Niagara peninsula, had been settled by large numbers of Americans who were expected to welcome annexation by their homeland. Victory would be, as former President Thomas Jefferson predicted, "a mere matter of marching."

If there was any resistance, the American generals thought it would be easy to crush. The colonies of British North America should not have had a chance in a land war against the United States. The Americans had more than ten times their population and vastly superior resources. With Great Britain distracted fighting Napoleon in Europe, it seemed likely that at least Upper Canada – the colony that later became Ontario – would fall to the Americans. Geography made this British territory just north of the Great Lakes particularly vulnerable to conquest from the south. Its only line of supply and communication was the St. Lawrence River, which lay exposed to attack for much of its length just a short distance from the American border. If the Americans could sever this lifeline at any point, the fall of Upper Canada would be just a matter of time.

But Canada was saved by American ineptitude and dissension countered by British competence and initiative. Regional variations in American support for the conflict made a critical difference. It was the midwest states that were most eager to fight, and they provided a large pool of manpower for operations in the Detroit area. This meant that the American army would spend most of its time snapping at Upper Canada' s hindquarters rather than going for the jugular. At first it could only do so with poorly trained militia and green volunteers. Early in the war the American army might have been capable of "a mere matter of marching," but it was ill-prepared to fight veteran European troops.

The British redcoats based in Canada were the superior soldiers, but there were only 1,600 of them. Their commander, Major-General Isaac Brock, knew he could count on the support of the native nations, who had long been Britain's allies, but he had reason to fear that the Americans were right about the loyalty of the Canadian population. When he called out the militia to defend the province, some units refused to muster, while others that did showed signs of being unreliable. The odds against them were daunting.

After sizing up the situation, Brock decided that the best defence was a good offence. He would "speak loud and look big" in the hope that the

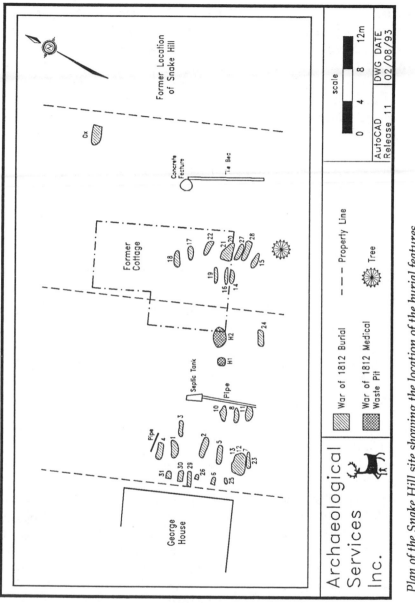

Plan of the Snake Hill site showing the location of the burial features.

unreliable elements of the population would at least remain neutral while the outcome hung in the balance. He would also strike at the Americans before they had a chance to organize their superior resources, and then try to keep them off-balance for as long as possible. Ultimately, most of the militia proved to be loyal, and Brock's aggressive plan worked. The opening engagements of the war brought some surprising American reverses. Brock himself was killed in the Battle of Queenston Heights in 1812, but his strategy lived on, and the British were able to inflict a series of embarrassing defeats on their would-be invaders during the first two years of the war.

For the Americans the only good consequence of these initial failures was that they learned from their mistakes. Inept old men in the American command were replaced by younger, tougher, and more enterprising commanders. By 1814 the American army had become a well-trained, efficient military machine, and as a result the fighting on the Niagara frontier that summer was bloodier than ever. Although neither side ever fielded more than 4,000 men at any one time in those months, over 2,400 British and 1,800 Americans were killed or wounded. These devastating casualty rates came in a campaign that ranged the length of the Niagara frontier and included desperate battles at Chippawa, Lundy's Lane and Fort Erie itself.

Some of the participants in those battles now rested at 659 Lakeshore Road, Fort Erie, Ontario, where every morning the archaeological team came to work with them. It was a professional relationship: each patient lay on his back while Williamson or one of his colleagues probed significant aspects of his past.

The focus of the dig was shifting from an extensive search of the site to an intensive scrutiny of each of its features. When the archaeologists first located a specific burial, they removed only as much dirt as was necessary to identify its contents. This ensured that the bones would be preserved just as they had been found until they could be given an archaeologist's full attention. Before detailed work commenced, a trench was dug around the burial feature to make it easier to stand or kneel alongside. As this process was repeated on one skeleton after another it became convenient to remove the earth between the trenches as well to facilitate movement around each group of burials. The floor of operations descended, leaving the skeletons lying on elevated pedestals of earth like stretcher cases in a hospital tent.

When studying a skeleton the archaeologists paid particular attention to the way each part of it rested – the "articulation" of the bones. The positioning of the body yielded critical information, and pains were taken to record it accurately. Once remains were fully exposed, a precise drawing

Burial 5 – note the "pedestal" of earth which facilitated the fieldwork.

of them was made. Then they were photographed in black-and-white and in colour. Sgt. Jay Llewellyn, a forensic photographer who had been loaned to the archaeological team by the U.S. Armed Forces Institute of Pathology, took dozens of rolls of film and a number of videotapes of the archaeologists at work.

The burials were in damp, sandy soil. It soon became clear that some of the bones were so wet and crumbly that they would be difficult to remove intact. As a precaution, Williamson had a physical anthropologist review each skeleton "*in situ*" (the archaeological term for "just as it was discovered") to ensure that no significant clues to age, sex, stature, or pathology would be destroyed *en route* to the lab. In the case of one burial, two conservators, Anne MacLaughlin and Julia Fenn from the Royal Ontario Museum, encased each of the crumbling bones in a plaster cast to ensure it remained intact in transit.

Williamson was also concerned about preserving metal artifacts. By this point they had found hundreds of buttons, as well as a spoon and a couple of musket tools. He invited another archaeological conservator, Charlotte Newton from the Canadian Conservation Institute, a federal agency in Ottawa, to visit the site to advise on their preservation. Buttons that were in good shape were wrapped in acid-free tissue and put in perforated plastic zip-lock bags for removal to Toronto. But the spoon, the

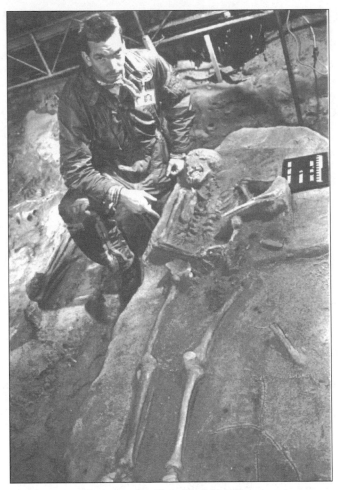

Photographer Sgt. Jay Llewellyn.

musket tools, and some of the buttons were in such delicate condition that small blocks of the soil containing them were lifted out to minimize their disturbance. These packages were secured within cotton gauze and paraffin wax, allowed to dry, then wrapped in a stretch gauze to secure them during transport.

To complicate matters, aboriginal artifacts were often found with the soldiers' remains. In the soils around some of the skeletons they found flint arrowheads, knives, and a cache of half-made tools dating to about 1,800 B.C. These items suggested that aboriginals had used the area as a source of stone for their tools and weapons. There was also evidence of an Iroquoian fishing camp at the site. But it was a relatively recent

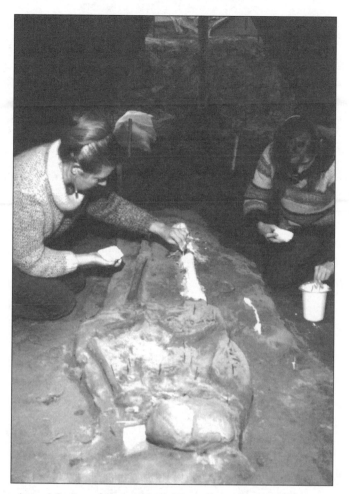

Anne MacLaughlin and Julia Fenn from the Royal Ontario Museum placing bones in plaster casts.

occupation – it appeared to be only about six hundred years old.

As the dig proceeded, the crowd by the roadside lent a sense of live theatre to the scene. The plot may not have unfolded at a dizzying pace, but at least the drama was real. Information on the latest developments on the site trickled out to the spectators in dribs and drabs, where it was circulated and embellished in a cycle of audience participation that renewed itself with each departure and arrival. Often a reporter or two was there as well, eager for news of the latest discovery or the newest theory. The U.S. public television network, PBS, sent a team to make a documentary about the dig.

Charlotte Newton conserving metal artifacts.

One of the weekly media conferences.

Weekly press conferences made the media less of a day-to-day nuisance, and its coverage was useful in that it raised the public profile of the dig and increased the probability of government funding. Williamson quickly became adept at providing journalists with various angles on the story to maintain their interest. He reported early on, for example, that the height of the skeletons was roughly the same as the average stature of modern American males. Since this contradicted the common belief that people were shorter two centuries ago, it received a lot of media play.

There were also contemporary aspects of the story for reporters to pursue. The owner of the lot on which the dig began was Vince Dunn, a high school art teacher, and he became a good source of "human interest" coverage. He explained to reporters that he was happy to co-operate with the dig because a tragedy in his past made him empathize with the dead soldiers. His twin brother, a NATO Starfighter pilot, had been killed twenty years before when his jet crashed into the North Sea. Dunn had been with him the night before he disappeared, but had never been able to learn anything about his death from the military. "I can just imagine what the families must have felt like when these guys didn't come back, because I know," Dunn told a reporter. "I hope if my brother's body is ever found washed up on some shore somewhere that somebody would look after it. That's where I felt a strong responsibility to these guys."[1] What was deeply

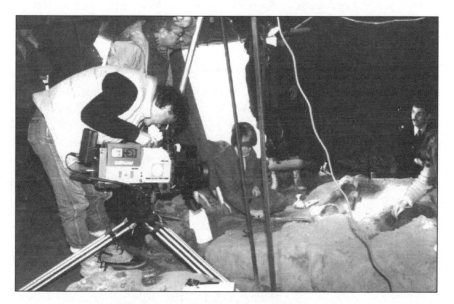

Dan Bjarnason (standing left), a CBC journalist,
interviewing Lieutenant Colonel Whitehorne (crouching right).

Remembrance Day wreath.

felt emotion for Dunn was good copy for the press. The archaeologists had allowed Dunn to observe the excavation and he was there almost every day. "You really get to know the skeletons and you start wondering who they were," he told reporters. On Remembrance Day he had laid a wreath at the site.

Another media diversion was canine rather than human. A dog trainer from Lockport, New York, had asked Williamson for a chance to test one of his protégés, a grave-sniffing Labrador, on the ancient burial site. At first Williamson was reluctant, but he finally agreed. Sheriff's Special Deputy William Tohurst showed up with Candy, a chocolate Lab, who proceeded to bark excitedly at all the right spots. She even "alerted" in an area that had yet to be checked. The media loved this episode; journalists were particularly delighted when more burials were later found at the site of the canine prediction. Williamson, the resident scientist, was asked to explain the dog's talent; he made a stab at it, suggesting that Candy might have smelled high concentrations of nitrogen or phosphorus produced by decaying bones.

What the media really wanted (despite these distractions) was a positive identification of the remains. If they could put names and faces on the skeletons, or even on just one skeleton, the story would really come alive. At first Williamson thought that letters, medical records, and enlistment papers might provide clues to physical characteristics that would be

Deputy William Tohurst, Dr. Ron Williamson, and Candy.

evident in the bones. "We have ... descriptions of past war trauma, missing front teeth, six foot one, stocky build, and a regiment," he told the press. "To a physical anthropologist, missing teeth, war wounds, consistent with the description, general reconstruction, and the button identifying the regiment will provide us with likely identification of the individual."

It would take some time to determine whether it would be possible to identify individuals, but it was relatively easy to reconstruct major events

Major General Jacob Brown.
Courtesy of Division of Armed Forces History,
Smithsonian Institution, Washington, D.C.

in the last few months of their lives. The soldiers who were buried at Snake Hill had survived a series of bloody battles before their luck finally ran out. Their commander had been Major General Jacob Brown, whose army had been based at Sackets Harbor at the east end of Lake Ontario early in 1814. The U.S. secretary of war had wanted Brown to attack Kingston, the British naval base and military stronghold across the lake. To mislead the British, he arranged for them to intercept a letter designed to reinforce their expectation of an American attack along the Niagara peninsula. But Brown did not feel he could rely on Commodore Chauncey, the commander of the American naval force on Lake Ontario, and without explanation he chose to attack where he had been intended to feint. He marched his men to the other end of Lake Ontario to launch an offensive at Niagara.

The secretary of war was surprised by Brown's action, but decided to make the best of a bad situation by planning a Niagara offensive in concert with attacks through the upper Great Lakes and the Champlain valley that year. The U.S. Navy's dominance on Lake Erie would allow him to concentrate troops in the Buffalo area. Without having to contest naval control of Lake Ontario, these forces could move east towards Burlington Heights, sever British western bases from their lifelines, and prepare for an overland assault on Kingston. At the very least they should be able to take the provincial capital of York (now Toronto) that summer.

The British had believed the false letter and were expecting trouble in Niagara, but they did not dare send all their men there. Instead, the British forces in the area were instructed to withdraw under attack, making things as difficult as possible for the invaders by fighting as they did so. At the mouth of the Niagara River, the garrisons at Fort George and Fort Niagara were expected to force the Americans to launch lengthy siege operations or, if they were bypassed, to serve as bases to harass the enemy rear.

Brown decided to cross the Niagara River at Fort Erie where his lines of supply would be short and secure. The first units of the invading army set out from near Buffalo shortly after midnight on 3 July 1814. It was raining steadily, but the operation went smoothly, if at times comically. Brigadier General Winfield Scott, a stern disciplinarian who commanded the first brigade, was eager to lead his troops ashore and leapt from his landing craft before it touched ground. Unfortunately, the water was over his head, and despite his lofty rank he sank, weighed down by sword, pistol, boots, and a heavy cloak. The oarsmen had to snag him with their boathooks and drag him, wet and steaming, back into the boat.

Brig. Gen. Winfield Scott.
Engraving by Thomas Gimbrede (1786-1866).
Reproduced by permission.
The National Portrait Gallery.
Smithsonian Institution, Washington, D.C.

Other than the embarrassment and indignity of this little mishap, Scott had a good night. The 137 British soldiers in Fort Erie put up only token resistance and then surrendered to the first wave of invaders. The landing operation continued well into the next morning until 3,500 men were assembled on the Canadian shore. The main force was divided into Scott's brigade and another commanded by Brigadier General Eleazar Ripley. Its backbone was its infantry regiments (the 9th, 11th, 21st, 22nd, 23rd, and 25th) and four batteries of artillery. There were also various special units: one company of light dragoons, another of engineers, 500 Pennsylvanian militia volunteers and 600 Iroquois. Later reinforcements would come from two more infantry regiments, the 17th and the 19th, along with 600 New York volunteers.

The Americans had not arrived unannounced. During their landing a mounted British patrol outside the fort escaped northward through the night to alert the main British army at Fort George. Major-General Phineas Riall, commander of the British forces on the Niagara Peninsula, was not unduly alarmed at the news. He had hoped that Fort Erie would hold longer than it did, but he was confident that his British regulars could handle the Americans. Although he had not had much combat experience, his superior at York, Major-General Gordon Drummond, had assured him that the American troops were no match for his redcoats. Riall gathered his men and set out to confront the invaders.

The cockiness of the British command was a product of pride and prejudice reinforced by observation and experience. In the early nineteenth century, armies were still fighting in a traditional eighteenth-century style dictated by the nature of their firearms. The infantryman loaded his musket from the muzzle by ramming powder charge and shot down the barrel with a rod. Then he poured a bit of gunpowder into the firing pan and aimed. When he pulled the trigger, a flintlock snapped down, producing a spark in the firing pan, which ignited the main charge and propelled the musketball towards its target. "Towards" was usually the best that could be expected: rifling had yet to be introduced and the smooth-bore musket was not terribly accurate. The sad fact was that, on his own, the average soldier could not shoot very often or very precisely.

These constraints dictated military tactics. Although loading and firing took only a few seconds, in the midst of a raging battle a few seconds were a lifetime. Soldiers had to be extremely well disciplined to resist the natural human impulse to break and run when exposed unarmed to enemy fire. They were organized into ranks that would fire at different times so that those who were reloading felt they had some protection. To offset the inaccuracy of the individual shot, ranks fired simultaneously in volleys that were designed to rip into enemy lines like giant shotgun blasts. Since this firing sequence required co-ordinated movements by hundreds of men, military drill emphasized the maintenance of tight formations through all of the complex manoeuvres needed to position an army in the field. Once facing the enemy, the ranks would load and fire in sequence. If things went well, the entire line would advance a few paces, halt, and repeat the process. As men fell wounded or dead, NCOs pushed replacements up from behind – at sword-point, if necessary – to close the ranks and re-form the line. When enemy troops were within a few yards, an aggressive commander might order a bayonet charge in the hope of breaking their line and driving them from the field.

Drummond had assured Riall that he could handle the Americans with fewer men because the superior training and battle experience of the British made all the difference in this type of warfare. Riall soon had a chance to see for himself. The two forces made contact along the river near Chippawa, a few kilometres upstream from Niagara Falls, on 4 July. The British had established themselves north of the mouth of the Chippawa River, and the American army came upon them as it followed the Niagara River downstream. In between the two armies lay cleared fields that stretched inland for half a mile from the river. The Americans stopped and camped behind a small stream known as Street's Creek (now Usher's Creek), about a mile south of the British positions.

Despite being outnumbered, Riall decided to attack the Americans while they were still relatively disorganized and before they received reinforcements. Early on the morning of 5 July he dispatched natives and militia through the woods to harass the enemy's flank. General Winfield Scott was in for another embarrassing brush with disaster. Confident that the smaller British force would await his attack, he had just sat down to breakfast in a Canadian farmhouse north of Street's Creek when hostile native warriors began to stream out of the nearby woods. He and his officers ran for their horses and barely managed to gallop to safety.

Back in the secure haven of his camp, Scott sent Pennsylvanian volunteers to skirmish with the British irregulars in the woods and turned his attention to arranging a belated Fourth of July dinner and dress parade for his men. But soon the festivities were interrupted by another surprise: the entire British army was advancing in a column across the Chippawa River. Unless Scott acted fast, the Pennsylvanians would be outflanked and decimated. Since his men were already formed for dress parade Scott was able to march them promptly across Street's Creek into a battle line.

Riall, seeing no sign of the blue uniforms of the regular American army, thought his opponents were all militia and brought his field guns into action anticipating a easy victory. In fact, a shortage of blue cloth had

Battle of Chippawa, "Those are regulars, by God!"
Courtesy U.S. Army, Centre of Military History.

forced the American army to issue grey uniforms to Brown's men. The British were facing regulars who had undergone months of rigorous and repetitive drill throughout the previous spring. Now their training was apparent as, under enemy artillery fire, they manoeuvred precisely into formation. Watching this feat, Riall realized he had been mistaken. "Those are regulars, by God!" he is reputed to have exclaimed.

No doubt many of the soldiers who would be buried at Snake Hill were in the American ranks that day. Some of them were militiamen, but most were regular soldiers. Many were just teenagers – mere boys who had been farmhands or apprentices a few months before. Fourteen was the official minimum age for a recruit, but there were drummer-boys in the American ranks who were as young as twelve. One can only imagine their worm's-eye view of the conflict.

Gut-wrenching fear must have seized the soldier entering his first battle. Responding instinctively to shouted orders, he marched beside his fellows into the meadow and wheeled into line. He could see the British guns surrounded by drifting smoke only 400 yards away, hear the sound of their explosions rumbling across the field and smell the gunpowder hanging in the air. He had already watched men topple where a blast had hit, down the line, and then a shot whistled in and smashed through three or four soldiers nearby with the sickening sound of iron crunching through flesh and bone. The screams that followed and the sight of guts and blood sent shivers up his spine, and he began to shake. A long swig from a flask of whisky helped numb his senses.

Finally the American guns were in position and returning the artillery fire. There was an explosion near one British gun that threw men and horses into great confusion. It looked as if one of the British ammunition carts had been hit, and after that the fire from their guns noticeably slackened. But then the enemy army began to move out from behind its gun positions and advance in column down the field directly towards the centre of the American line. An order was barked, and the American front rank knelt in firing position.

Then the real slaughter began. The American gunners switched to canister shot, tin containers filled with lead slugs the size of ping-pong balls that were effective in mowing down enemy troops at close range. They blasted away at the advancing column, tearing huge holes in its leading edge. Finally the command for the infantry to commence fire came down the line. After watching the enemy advance for so long, it was a relief for the regulars to lose themselves in the mechanics of their familiar drill. Their steady volleys were rewarded with the sight of ripples of tumbling bodies along the British ranks. Men lay screaming and dying in the

American ranks as well, but the line continued to load and fire in deadly concert.

The natural human impulse would have been to turn and run, but few soldiers did. It was more than a mercenary calculation of their odds of survival that kept them in their ranks. They had lived with each other for months, shared each others' lives and feelings, and developed an unspoken pact of mutual support. They would not abandon their brothers-in-arms in battle. To do so would bring a dishonour far deeper than mere cowardice.

The British kept coming. Their flanks were exposed to the fire of American lines folding around their far left and right, and they were losing men at every step. But still they moved forward. When they were two hundred yards away their leading officer signalled a charge and the red column burst forward like a cresting wave. But many began to stumble in the rough field, and the surge soon broke in the teeth of withering American infantry and artillery fire. A few redcoats made it to within eighty yards, but as they noticed their numbers dwindle they began to turn around and run away. The British general remained, waving his troops forward from horseback as he advanced. Suddenly everyone was taking shots at him; it seemed impossible that he was still mounted. The officer beside him was hit. He pulled up, looked around, and, as his predicament became clear, turned and followed his men from the field.

The Americans had won a terrible victory against good European troops. They had driven the British from the field after inflicting over five hundred casualties, and had lost only three hundred men themselves. Two days later the British army began to retreat northward to Fort George. Brown followed and paused at Queenston Heights until Commodore Chauncey arrived with the heavy guns he would need to besiege Fort George and the basic supplies he needed to feed and re-equip his men. For ten days he waited in vain. He tried to entice the British out of Fort George to fight, but they wisely sat tight and awaited reinforcements. Finally Brown gave up, withdrew to Chippawa, and contemplated his options. Should he forget about the British forts and advance on Burlington?

His options, limited to begin with, were quickly running out. Major-General Drummond had called out the Canadian militia from Long Point to the Bay of Quinte and was *en route* from York with these forces and all the regular infantry units he could spare. In the meantime a British column from Fort George was rumoured to be advancing up the American side of the Niagara River. Brown was alarmed because this advance jeopardized his source of supplies and he had no way of crossing the river to parry it. Opting for a counter-move that would force the British back, he dispatched General Scott's brigade from Chippawa to threaten Fort George.

Scott set off on 25 July, marching his brigade north along the Portage Road that ran parallel to the Niagara River. A road called Lundy's Lane crossed their path on a ridge just inland from the falls. The land on either side had been cleared for farming, and as his troops approached the bottom of the slope leading up to the church at the intersection they could see British troops and guns ranged along the high ground.

The British had only just arrived. Earlier that afternoon a small force under General Riall had been in the area, and he had begun to withdraw to avoid the larger American army. But as he did he ran into the British reinforcements under Drummond arriving from Burlington. The combined British forces quickly moved south and ran their guns to the top of the ridge by Lundy's Lane. Just a few minutes later Scott's brigade marched into view. He dispatched some skirmishing parties to feel out the situation and found himself in a ticklish position. The British outnumbered him and held the better position, yet he could not retreat without exposing his army to an attack from behind. Deciding that his best chance lay in a prompt, aggressive attack, he sent for reinforcements and began to deploy for battle.

At about six in the evening the 11th and 22nd infantry regiments advanced up the hill, right into the centre of the British lines. This time it was the British gunners' turn to mow down enemy infantry. Despite heavy losses Scott's troops pressed on, closing to hand-to-hand combat in many places. But they could not dislodge the British from the hill. Initially things went better on the eastern flank. There the American 25th Infantry managed to evade British detection by circling through the woods on the right side of the Portage Road and outflanking the left side of the British line. They received a welcoming gift – General Riall, who had been wounded in the arm, was delivered into their lines by confused stretcher bearers. Nevertheless, the British adjusted to the new threat and blocked them from a further advance.

Dusk was falling, but on the field of battle the day was not yet decided. The rest of the American army under Brown had arrived to reinforce Scott at around seven o'clock. There was a lull in the fighting as the American officers pondered their next move. In the ranks there was determination but no elation. The British guns on the hill were their obvious objective, but the task of capturing them was daunting. In the meantime the British received reinforcements from Burlington.

BURIAL 5

T his skeleton showed clear signs of a traumatic death. An iron ball was found next to his right shoulder blade, a fragment of brick rested along his upper spine, and there was damage to one of the ribs of his lower right back. These multiple injuries may have occurred simultaneously as the result of a nearby explosion.

There was other evidence that made Burial 5 particularly interesting. Tests showed that he had been about twenty years old, five feet five inches tall (164.8 cm), and may not have been an American by birth. His bones had isotope values that suggested European origins, and high lead levels, which pointed to either an upper-class background or an occupation involving work with lead, such as silversmithing. His skull was slightly smaller than the North American average and his teeth showed signs of disease or malnutrition in infancy.

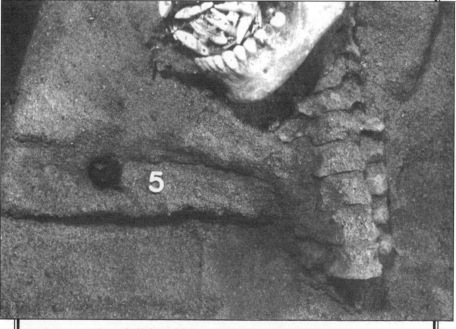

Iron ball found below right shoulder of Burial 5.

His body had been deposited in a fairly wide grave that was probably dug when there was time to ensure a spacious fit. The grave cut through a deposit of prehistoric native artifacts, which included a stone flaking tool, animal bones, charcoal and flint. It also intersected a medical waste pit.

Since no buttons were found with his skeleton, this soldier might have been hospitalized for some time before his death. A copper pin, found resting against his breastbone, might have been used during the application of a bandage to a wound. His grave contained something extra: an additional forearm and hand lay beside his right elbow. They came from a very young teenager and appeared to have been amputated because of a fracture or projectile injury.

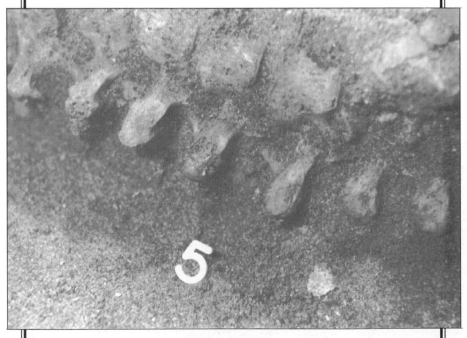

Brick fragment found embedded in vertebral column.

Eventually the orders came down. The 23rd and the 1st regiments were sent back up the middle of the southern slope to divert the enemy's attention while Ripley's brigade crept up the hill under cover of darkness. It worked. Ripley's men escaped detection until they were just a few yards away from the British artillery, then charged, bayoneting the British gunners in the act of loading. Behind them other troops poured in to secure their foothold. Soon the high ground and the prized guns were securely in American hands. It was the high tide of the American campaign of 1814.

For the American soldiers, now on the defensive, the rest of that night was a murderous nightmare. Soon after they reached the hilltop the British launched a determined counterattack. The U.S. soldiers heard them coming, but they couldn't see them, and could only aim at the musket flashes that pierced the gloom on the slope below. Then the British charged, and there was confused and desperate hand-to-hand combat. Men stood toe to toe, slashing at one another with eighteen-inch bayonets and smashing skulls with gun butts. In the darkness it was hard to tell a shadow from an enemy soldier and an enemy soldier from a friend. Three times the British charged, but the Americans held the hill. Then General Brown, aware that his men were exhausted and running short of ammunition and water, decided to withdraw, taking the captured guns with him. The operation was timed so poorly that before the guns could be dragged away the British recaptured the top of the ridge. The Americans had thrown away both the high ground and the heavy artillery that they had won at such cost.

When morning broke the British were atop the hill amidst hundreds of bodies. The dead of both armies lay in mounds, intermingled with lifeless horses and discarded equipment. The British fighting strength was reduced by 876; the Americans reported 861 casualties and missing men. Attrition in the U.S. officer ranks was particularly high, with Generals Brown and Scott included among the wounded. The Americans withdrew to Chippawa, then, after assessing their remaining strength, retreated all the way back to Fort Erie. There General Ripley began preparing to defend the fort against a British siege. The British, badly mauled themselves, were slow in pursuit. Drummond's men were exhausted, and supplies and heavy guns had to be brought up. This gave the Americans time to strengthen their fortifications, including the battery at Snake Hill that anchored their defensive line by the lake.

The men who would end up dead and buried near the Snake Hill battery were no doubt grateful to march back to the relative safety of the fort. They had survived a bloody campaign in enemy territory and now seemed close to returning to their homeland. They could not know that they had arrived at the place, if not the time, of their death. If they had they might have been comforted to know that they had already established a place for themselves in American military lore. The victory over the British at the Battle of Chippawa was a glorious moment that the American army would always remember. It is commemorated to this day by the grey uniforms worn by West Point cadets, and in many an army barracks there hangs a picture of the grey-clad soldiers in action, underscored by the caption "Those are regulars, by God!" The American army made good use of its history.

Indeed, the Snake Hill archaeological dig was a vivid testament to the U.S. Army's appreciation of its past. It was considered a project of importance in the highest ranks of the army command. General Quinn Becker, Surgeon-General of the army, had authorized the U.S. military's support of the dig. He took a very real, personal interest in the outcome. One day a van arrived from the Buffalo airport and disgorged the general and a half-dozen of his staff. He wanted to take a look at the site, and had flown up from Washington for the afternoon with his entourage for a quick tour. Lieutenant Colonel Trotter and Lieutenant-Colonel Daryl Prosser of the Canadian Armed Forces were there to greet him with all the military ceremony due an officer of his elevated rank. Williamson, less formally attired in jeans, work boots, and the ubiquitous ASI cap, led a procession of officers in uniforms with razor-sharp creases and shoes that gleamed almost as brightly as their ribbons. The general asked numerous astute questions, his subordinates remained respectfully attentive but mute, and after a two-hour visit they all got back in the van and returned to Washington.

General Becker was just one of a parade of VIPs that Williamson found himself escorting around the dig. The skeletons had become celebrities, and people wanted to meet them. Bureaucrats and politicians from all levels and departments of government arrived to see first hand what they were being asked to fund. Williamson was a conscientious tour guide. One day it was the head of the U.S. Armed Forces Institute of Pathology, the next day a local politician. There was even Lois Maxwell (alias Miss Moneypenny, Agent 007's favourite secretary), now a columnist for the Toronto *Sun*. On another occasion it was a local priest who claimed it was his spiritual duty to inspect the remains.

Despite such diversions the archaeological work continued at a steady pace. Most of the skeletons had been fully exposed and the archaeologists were awaiting legal permission to remove the bodies from the ground. At the same time some new burials came to light as they did a final sweep

General Quinn Becker (far right), Surgeon-General of the United States Army, and entourage visiting the site, accompanied by Lt.-Col. Darryl Prosser (far left) of the Canadian army.

around the edges of the site. Beyond the eastern end of the cemetery, half-way to the road, a larger than usual burial shaft was uncovered. Closer examination revealed bones that turned out to be the remains of an ox. But this was not the only surprise. Back to the west, they examined the thin strip of land between the first burial and the George property line and discovered six more graves, or parts of graves. Excavation revealed that each contained a portion of a skeleton that had been bisected by the excavation trench for the George house.

Altogether the dig had uncovered thirty-one human skeletons, one ox skeleton, three medical waste pits, 440 buttons, some straight pins, a handful of musket-shot, a pewter spoon, assorted military paraphernalia, and a wisp of hair. But by the beginning of December they were no closer to identifying individual skeletons. Williamson would later note that his job "was to insure that they didn't send a Brit back to a U.S. cemetery."[2] But this required only a determination of nationality, not individuals' names.

In fact, the American army was not eager for anything more. The positive identification of individuals would have created a colossal headache for Trotter and his department. Under U.S. law, dead soldiers' relatives had a right to determine their place of burial. Usually this compassionate policy made sense, but in the Snake Hill case it opened up a bottomless can of worms. After two centuries, descendants of the dead could number in the thousands. Tracing the relatives of just one individual, or even verifying the claims of anyone who came forward and claimed to be related, would involve massive genealogical research. And what if various branches of a family disagreed about what to do with their great-great-great-grandfather? The prospect was a bureaucratic nightmare. It would be far simpler not to know and to rebury all the skeletons in a national military cemetery. It would be far more symbolic if they remained anonymous and were buried with a ceremony honouring all War of 1812 soldiers whose fates were unknown.

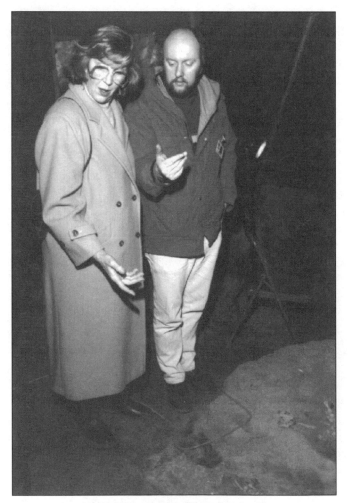

Dr. Williamson and Lois Maxwell.

Beverly Garner and Andrew Clish working on Burial 2.

Deborah Steiss working on burials 7, 12, and 13 – "The Three Lads."

Ox burial.

By the end of November much of the *in situ* archaeological study was completed. But the exposed skeletons had to remain where they were until the archaelogists received legal permission to exhume the bones. The coroner's approval finally came, allowing this final stage of the dig to commence in the first week of December. It was a painstaking process. Each bone was removed separately, wrapped in paper towelling, then labelled and placed in a paper bag within a steel-reinforced cardboard container for shipment to Toronto. It took a pair of archaeologists the better part of a day to completely disinter one skeleton, and it was expected that the entire process would take another week and a half. Everyone on the team was hoping they could go home for Christmas with the dig wrapped up.

Mother Nature gave this schedule an unexpected push forward. On Monday 7 December, the weather report was ominous. Already the skies were a dirty grey, and the winds on the lake were whipping up whitecaps that tumbled powerfully to shore a few metres from the tents. At first the archaeologists were not too worried. The heavy-duty canvas seemed secure against the wind and would protect the site from the rain. But locals, familiar with the area, began to voice concerns. The weather had been remarkably good to date, but in previous years late fall storms had driven waves over low-lying lakeshore properties. Just the year before, Lakeshore Road had been flooded where it ran closer to the lake just a few hundred

Tent by the George property containing graves bisected by the construction trench.

A number of fully exposed skeletons on the west side of the site.

metres eastward. If similar conditions developed there was a good possibility that rising water levels and high waves could reach as far as the dig and flood it out.

Town officials and concerned residents began to drop by to warn the team of this danger, and Williamson listened with growing unease. He did not want to be remembered as a *marine* archaeologist. Flooding would cause irreversible damage, and the main group of burials on the Dunn property was in a low-lying area that was particularly vulnerable. By late afternoon the waves were creeping noticeably closer and the weather office was predicting a severe storm. It was time for crisis management – or at least more crisis management than usual. The archaeologists met as dusk fell and agreed that before the storm hit its peak they should try to remove any skeletons that were in danger. They sent out for pizza and set to work. The dozen skeletons on the Dunn lot were in the most danger. They were in a race against the clock, yet they had to perform each exhumation in as exacting a fashion as usual. As the wind rose to a howl and plucked away at the tent flaps, Andrew Clish and Rob MacDonald ran around securing guy lines and checking fasteners. Outside, a crew sent by the town began building a wall of sandbags to hold back the waves and refilling side-trenches that would have conducted water into the main excavation.

On they worked into the night. Their spirits were lifted by the arrival of Doug Owsley, a senior physical anthropologist from the Smithsonian who had been helping with the project. Owsley had just arrived in Buffalo that evening and immediately came to the site to help with the work. Other omens, such as the toppling of the portable toilet by a particularly vicious gust of wind, were more difficult to interpret. At midnight they still had five skeletons to remove, and the storm was growing stronger still. Two hours later the waves were hitting the sandbags only twenty feet from the tent wall. Three skeletons remained. As they reached the third they became conscious that the storm was abating. The wind slackened appreciably and the waves were no longer cresting so high on the shore. They finished work on the last skeleton in any case and wearily set out homeward at 4 a.m. Moments after they rounded a corner down the road, a tree toppled over the hydro lines and the lights went out behind them.

It was a dramatic finale to the Snake Hill dig. The removal of the remaining bones was inevitably something of an anticlimax. The burst of work prompted by the crisis had ensured that all the archaeological field work would be finished by Christmas; by the third week of December the dig was winding up. The site was left looking as barren, muddy, and criss-

BURIAL 19

T his soldier had a stylish burial compared to most of his comrades-in-arms: like Burial 4, he was interred in a coffin. Perhaps this confused those who had buried him, because his head had been placed in the east end of the grave rather than the west. But this was not the only interesting feature of this burial. His skeleton displayed evidence of the most traumatic injury to be seen among the entire group of Snake Hill skeletons. In his lower left abdomen there was an enormous gap. It looked as if he had taken a direct hit from a cannonball. His hips and legs were broken, probably as a result of the impact higher up on his body. Having died instantly, he was still fully dressed and his feet had been bound to make his corpse easier to carry to the cemetery. He had been about twenty-three years old and five feet seven inches (171.4 cm) in height.

It is probable that this soldier was in the militia. The buttons found in the grave were civilian rather than military in style. He seemed to have been buried wearing ordinary clothes, including a shirt, a jacket or vest, and trousers. The buttons provided the clearest evidence of a militia casualty in the Snake Hill cemetery.

Burial 19 – note the gap above the pelvis.

crossed by trenches as a First World War battlefield. But now that it had surrendered its secrets, bulldozers would come to restore its suburban equilibrium. In the meantime the bones and artifacts had all been shipped to Toronto – or York, as it had been known in 1814 – where they would be studied intensively over the next few months. Some of General Brown's soldiers had finally reached one of their military objectives, albeit in rougher shape and a little later than their commander had hoped.

Chapter 3

THE ARCHIVES AND
THE LABORATORY

"I'm hopping mad," Ron Williamson told the reporter from the Hamilton *Spectator*. It was early February 1988, six weeks after the dig had ended. The media were eager for more news about the project, but a lack of funding was still holding things up. Bones and artifacts were sitting in boxes at the ASI offices and the Royal Ontario Museum in Toronto, waiting for examination and conservation. But without assurances that someone would pay for the cost of the work, the project team could do nothing. Williamson had decided it was time to call the newspapers and put some media pressure on the Canadian government. "The American government quickly committed itself to funding its fair share and they're expecting to pay a substantial amount," he continued, "but it's highly embarrassing – it's a national crime that our government hasn't been able to make the same commitment."[1]

Ontario at least was doing its part. Premier David Peterson had invited the Town of Fort Erie to apply for provincial funding, and a $35,000 grant from the province's Community Facility Improvement Program had come through just the day before. But more money was urgently needed. The project had to be completed within three of four months at the most, for pressing reasons both legal and political. The legal time constraint was the Coroner's Act, which limited the period allowed for scientific examination of exhumed bones. The political difficulty was that the town of Fort Erie and the American army had both become interested in holding a repatriation ceremony for any identifiably American soldiers during Fort Erie's Friendship Festival, an annual 1–4 July celebration started just the year before to celebrate Canadian-American amity and attract some tourist dollars into the anaemic local economy. A committee including representatives from the town and the U.S. and Canadian military had been formed to plan the event.

That meant that there were only four months left to establish the nationality of the victims. In this time the project team was determined to find out as much as it could about the bones. Even information that did not seem relevant had to be noted and retained: it might provide answers to questions that could come up later, answers that could shed more light on the background of the soldiers and advance different fields of knowledge. The team needed time to measure, test, and analyse the skeletons from every conceivable angle. And it had to be done now. Once the current opportunity passed there would never be a second chance.

Williamson's pointed messages to the Canadian government were about as effective as a mouse kicking an elephant, but when the United States Army decided to get Ottawa's attention, things began to happen. Using its political influence in Washington, the army pushed for action through diplomatic channels. The U.S. embassy in Ottawa raised the Snake Hill problem with the Prime Minister's Office, and this high-level intercession finally jolted the federal government into action. By early March, Williamson was assured of federal funding and was able to shift the second stage of the project into high gear.

In the meantime, the Royal Ontario Museum, the Canadian Conservation Institute, and the Ontario Ministry of Culture and Communications had performed preliminary conservation work on some of the artifacts from the dig. The metal ones were cleaned and kept as dry as possible. The odd bits of cloth that had been found were also cleaned and mounted in a way that would protect them through study and storage. The fragments of wood from decayed coffins required quite different treatment. It was important that they remain as moist as they had been when they were found so that they would not fall apart. They also had to be cool to discourage mould and dark to prevent algae growth. Isopropanol was applied to further inhibit biological activity. Once all the artifacts had been treated, they were sent to the ASI offices for cataloguing and analysis. There, on the second floor of a Victorian brick building at a busy intersection near the University of Toronto, the ASI team grappled with the daunting task of making sense of the evidence it had amassed. The archaeologists began by classifying the over four hundred buttons by type and analysing how they were distributed around the skeletons to see what they could contribute to an understanding of who the soldiers were and how they died.

At the same time, the bones were distributed to various scientists for analysis of their size, shape, and chemical composition. A number of physical anthropologists – Dr. Douglas Owsley of the Smithsonian Institution in Washington, Dr. Marc Micozzi of the National Museum of Health and Medicine (part of the Armed Forces Institute of Pathology), and Dr. Jerry Cybulski of Canada's National Museum of Civilization in Ottawa – had been involved with the project from its earliest stages. Cybulski had assumed leadership of the team during the dig. The data and samples they collected would be subjected to exacting scholarly analysis in the months to come. Dr. Susan Pfeiffer, a physical anthropologist at the University of Guelph in Ontario, later assumed responsibility for co-ordinating further laboratory research on the bones. Pfeiffer would perform some of the analysis herself and recruit qualified experts who had access to the necessary equipment for the rest.

Osteobiography, the analysis of bones, is often a useful adjunct of archaeological inquiry. Usually it is associated with physical anthropology, but it can also be a multi-disciplinary enterprise involving medical researchers, biochemists, and forensic scientists. In osteobiography, every bone is seen as a unique product of its owner's particular genetic make-up and environmental experience. Individual samples are examined for their own unique characteristics, but each also contributes to the general knowledge of human evolution. For example, the physical anthropologists who worked on the Snake Hill project were interested in the size of the soldiers' skulls as an indicator of how cranial size and shape had changed over the past two centuries. They found that the Snake Hill soldiers had generally had smaller skulls than modern North Americans. In part this may have been due to the relative youth of some of the victims, but there was still a difference significant enough to support the belief that skull sizes have increased in recent history, especially front to back. Still, it had to be kept in mind that the Snake Hill skeletons were not typical of their contemporaries. Their age, sex, size, and health had been criteria in their selection for duty.

Conclusions could not be drawn with absolute certainty on the evidence of the bones alone, but the scientific tests were nevertheless invaluable means of testing historical and archaeological evidence. For example,

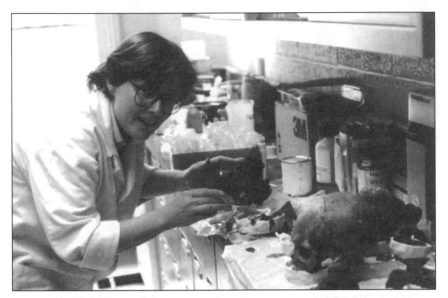

Dr. Susan Pfeiffer, at work at the University of Guelph.

matters as basic as the sex of the Snake Hill skeletons had to be settled. It was natural to assume that they were men because buttons from army uniforms were found in the graves. Yet some of the skeletons had slight frames. Were they the remains of adolescent males, or of women?

The latter possibility wasn't entirely out of the question. Armies of the day commonly had camp followers. Although there was no precise account of any women accompanying the American army on its march that summer, their presence was recorded after the army retreated from Lundy's Lane to Fort Erie. In several cases the quartermaster noted that local women or the wives of soldiers were hired to cook for different army units. In one case two people described as "Canadian women" were issued flour. Entries on the vouchers submitted by rations contractors also indicated that people classed as "indigent families" and "refugees" were present at Fort Erie at various times. These encounters were recorded mostly in July and October, periods when the tides of war made it most convenient for American sympathizers in Canada to seek asylum in the fort before crossing to the U.S. Occasionally the relatives of dead soldiers came to Fort Erie to settle the deceased's accounts. The wife of a 23rd Infantry soldier killed at Lundy's Lane, for example, was at the fort on 17 October. She drew her late husband's back pay from the regimental paymaster and collected his property from his old company. Her visit from West Point, N.Y., was not viewed as unusual. There were two women serving as hospital matrons and one as laundress in each army regiment at Fort Erie. In his work in the archives, Whitehorne found that at least one hospital matron drew pay at Fort Erie, rather than Buffalo, throughout the campaign. At one point General Brown ordered all women attached to the army to return to Buffalo to work at the hospital there, but regimental surgeons protested that this would drastically lower the level of care for the sick and wounded in the field hospitals. Thus a matron and a laundress were allowed to remain as long as the regimental hospitals were in operation.

In short, the verified presence of women at Fort Erie raised the possibility that some of the Snake Hill skeletons could be female. Dr. Shelley Saunders, a physical anthropologist attached to McMaster University and the Royal Ontario Museum, conducted the sex determination study of the bones. Saunders used the two most reliable techniques available: measurement of the lower leg bone and visual assessment of the skull and the hips. Neither method is completely foolproof. Precise measurements require complete and undamaged bones, which even then can only be compared to a reference data base that isn't comprehensive enough to satisfy the strictures of statistical science. The visual method, on the other hand, is inherently subjective, and consequently somewhat susceptible to the influence of preconceived expectations. To be safe, both methods were applied to the Snake Hill skeletons. On the basis of visual criteria, those Snake Hill skeletons with preserved pelvic bones all appeared to be male. The skulls all exhibited male characteristics too. In addition, most of the lower leg bones were too long to be female. Only two had skeletal features small enough to be in doubt, and they were identified as male on the basis of pelvic criteria.

Thus, historical evidence established a possibility – that not all the dead had been men – that was then ruled out by scientific evidence. It was an effective demonstration of how these different sources of evidence could combine to produce conclusions with greater certainty. As project leader, Williamson was at the confluence of three different streams of information: the historical, the archaeological, and the osteobiographical. It was a fascinating position, for it meant that he was the first to see the similarities in the pictures sketched by the different sources.

The historical evidence was flowing in steadily from Lieutenant Colonel Whitehorne in Washington. He had not been held up by the funding problems that plagued his Canadian colleagues because he was paid by the American army and his research expenses were modest. Whitehorne's experience as an American military historian gave him a huge head start in researching the subject. It wasn't that he knew everything about the 1814 campaign. No one did. But he knew something just as valuable: how to find what he needed to know.

The inchoate raw material of a nation's historical consciousness sits in cardboard boxes on the storage shelves of archives. The Snake Hill soldiers fought and died on British soil, but the story of their final days was retained in official records in their homeland. Whitehorne's familiarity with American military archives meant that he already knew where to go, who to ask, and what to look for to find out as much as possible about the background of the Snake Hill victims. He had to rely on primary sources such as military archives because secondary sources were less than reliable on a topic this specific. Sometimes other researchers' conclusions were simply wrong, at other times they were quick overviews that distorted the story. A few soldiers' memoirs conveyed some of the flavour of the campaign, but they were neither complete nor reliable. Historical accuracy required the use of documentary sources.

Fortunately for the historian, armies are huge bureaucracies. Even in its relative infancy the U.S. Army generated reams of paper. Many War of 1814 records had been stored in the east wing of the White House and had gone up in flames when the British torched the presidential residence late in the war. Others had been saved and stored but were inaccessible because they had never been catalogued. Still, the National Archives in Washington, D.C., had hundreds of feet of shelves laden with War of 1812 documents that had been both saved and indexed.

Finding the few that were relevant to Snake Hill was no simple matter. After checking through dozens of potential sources, Whitehorne began to concentrate on a few of the most promising, particularly those from the office of the adjutant general, the paymaster general, veterans' administration and the different contemporary army commands. Many of the boxes he called up had never been cracked open by a researcher. These records held a variety of information on General Jacob Brown's army, including personnel registers, purchase orders, requisitions for supplies, financial records, War Department correspondence, and commanders' reports. From these basic documents left by those responsible for the daily operations of the army, Whitehorne began to piece together a more complete account of the experience of the Snake Hill soldiers.

The picture that emerged both enlarged and corrected the story told in the history books. It was common knowledge – a matter of legend – that Brown's army of 1814 had been better drilled than its predecessors and that its superb training accounted for much of its success at Chippawa. But Whitehorne began to discover just how onerous and rigorous that training process had been. When Brown's troops had settled into camp in the Flint Hall area north of Buffalo in the spring of 1814, Brigadier General Winfield Scott took command of their training. Scott was a notorious disciplinarian who would later be nicknamed "Old Fuss and Feathers" for his conviction that military genius is in the details. In 1814 he first showed his true colours by whipping Brown's army into the best force fielded by the Americans during the war.

Scott had a three-pronged approach: drill, drill, and more drill. The War Department had no comprehensive training manual, so he adopted a standard French text and taught his officers by it. They in turn trained the men. He required his regimental commanders to supervise a minimum of four hours of squad and platoon drill each morning. Once the men had mastered the basics, developed a rhythm, and begun to respond to orders instinctually, they were introduced to more difficult operations, such as firing in three ranks. At the same time they were marched in ever bigger units to familiarize them with the mass manoeuvres required in the field. Volunteer units, like the Philadelphia militia who joined the command in mid-June, were subjected to the same routine. Daily battalion and company drills, sometimes conducted by Scott himself, were supplemented by a full field inspection of the entire force every Sunday.

It wasn't much fun for the men. By June, when the drill schedule was expanded again, the average soldier's day began at sunrise, when he was expected to turn out armed and in uniform to perform two hours of squad and company drill. A short breakfast break was followed by more of the same until noon. Tramping around under the hot sun, loaded down with fifty pounds of musket, pack, and equipment, was exhausting work. For a man used to a certain freedom of action, it was also an incredibly tedious, boring, and repressive regimen. Time passed with agonizing slowness, sweat tickled the skin, and the wool uniform chafed. Yet there was no stopping to stretch or mop one's brow without an officer's permission. Eventually noon would arrive with the long-anticipated relief of dinner and some discretionary time. But at 3 p.m., it was back to the parade ground for four hours of battalion drill. Finally came the evening oasis – an interlude of supper and free time. Still, one's kit had to be kept in order, and it was lights out at 9 p.m. The next day it was the same thing all over again – day after exhausting day, week after boring week. Not surprisingly, there was griping in the ranks about the constant drudgery. But discipline improved when Scott executed four would-be deserters by firing squad.

All of this training was necessary to transform a chaotic rabble into a disciplined and responsive military machine. By late June, the American command was drilling the entire army at once, giving field officers experience handling the full force in action. Scott was pleased with their progress. Farm boys, street urchins, and shop clerks alike were starting to behave like soldiers. The burden of constant training became bearable as they began to cultivate a perverse pride in their common privation, even to celebrate it in obscene and blustering marching songs that symbolized their new-found sense of collective strength. "They began to perceive why they had been made to fag so long at the drill of the soldier, the company, and the battalion," Scott recalled, "Confidence, the dawn of victory, inspired the whole line."

Williamson examined Whitehorne's reports on the soldiers' training with interest because of the light they shed on the scientific results he was receiving. For example, a team of Washington physical anthropologists, including Doug Owsley and Robert Mann of the Smithsonian Institution and Sean Murphy and Paul Sledzik of the National Museum of Health and Medicine of the Armed Forces Institute of Pathology, had examined the bones, looking for evidence of injury and disease in the Snake Hill skeletons. They had become convinced that the men had been subjected to a great deal of physical stress. There were signs of premature arthritis in relatively young skeletal remains. Leg bones showed fatigue fractures that could have resulted from extensive marching under heavy loads. All of this was consistent with Whitehorne's report of the intense training the American soldiers had undergone that spring, not to mention the rigours of the campaign that followed.

Whitehorne was soon discovering that the campaign itself had also been far more onerous than hitherto appreciated. The marching and the fighting at Chippawa and Lundy's Lane had been bad enough, but the worst physical toil came after the American army retreated to Fort Erie. The Americans had left behind a small garrison to hold the fort and improve upon its rudimentary defences. These men had done what they could, but it was not enough to provide security for the army which retreated there on 27 July. Protected only by the unfinished earthworks and weak batteries of Fort Erie, the invaders were in a precarious position. If the British army arrived, they would find themselves exposed and out-numbered, with their backs to the water.

Nevertheless, the army command was unwilling to abandon its foothold in enemy territory. Instead, the Americans launched a frantic effort to shore up their defences before they were attacked. A whole new defensive line was needed beyond the fort to allow the entire army protection and freedom of movement. They laid out plans for a thirty-acre fortified camp with new batteries to provide protection along its extended perimeter. To the north and east a short defensive line between the fort and the lake would be secured by the Douglass battery (batteries were

Old Fort Erie during the siege.
From **The Pictorial Field-Book of the War of 1812** *by Benson J. Lossing*
(New York: Harper & Brothers, 1868).

named after their commanding officers). To the southwest an ambitious 800-yard breastwork would be anchored at the lake's edge by the Towson battery on the low sandy mound known as Snake Hill. In between, but closer to the fort, two smaller gun emplacements were started: Fontaine's battery close to the fort and Biddle's battery 250 yards further south. The American command was also determined to bolster the flimsy fortifications of the uncompleted fort itself, particularly its makeshift western stockade. Between these strong-points they would build up as elaborate a defensive line for infantry as time allowed.

The American plans were ambitious and they didn't have much time. But they did have 2,800 men and access to supplies across the river. Once again, Scott's concern for details proved invaluable. He had anticipated such a situation the previous spring by having hand-picked soldiers from each company equipped with saws, spades, and axes. These "pioneers," as they were called, had been specially trained for constructing fortifications. Now each was assigned a work party of regular soldiers. Under the supervision of military engineers, they set to work on the new defences.

They had their work cut out for them. There were batteries to be built up out of earth and timber and guns to be hauled into place. There were breastworks to construct and ditches to dig. These tasks involved hauling in timbers to frame rough parapet walls, then shovelling dirt by hand to make ditches in front and walls behind. Beyond the outer rim of the ditch other work parties dragged in tree limbs, saplings, and brush, sharpened their ends to points, and arranged them outward towards the enemy. This created what was called an "abattis," early nineteenth-century warfare's version of barbed wire. There was also work to be done behind the lines: setting up camp, digging traverses, hauling in supplies. At the fort itself they built up the western walls with new earthworks, set up more gun emplacements, and began work on a blockhouse to connect the two redoubts. Each work party put in an eight-hour shift of bone-numbing toil every day, and the shifts were rotated around the clock. Day after day the American soldiers slaved away, knowing that their lives were, quite literally, on the line.

At the same time, the Americans requisitioned as much heavy artillery as they could find in western New York. Four twelve-pounders with solid, shrapnel, and canister rounds, and twenty-five barrels of gunpowder were shipped from Batavia. Nearly all of the ammunition, rifles, and sabres in stock at Fort Schlosser on the east bank of the Niagara were sent over, along with its only ten-pound mortar. Five eighteen-pounders at Oswego and 600 solid shot sent there from Sackets Harbor were shipped as well. Some of this heterogeneous collection of artillery went to defend Black

Rock on the American side of the river, but most became part of the heavy defences of Fort Erie.

These herculean efforts set the stage for the only full-scale siege of the war. Luckily for the Americans, the British took their time in pursuing them from Lundy's Lane. They had regrouped and waited for reinforcements before moving south. The main British army finally appeared at Fort Erie on 2 August, the very day that the guns for Douglass's battery were hauled into position. Captain Towson's battery at Snake Hill received part of its armament the next day.

The British army set up camp two miles north and its engineers soon began building a battery only 1,000 yards from the fort.

Captain Nathan Towson.
Courtesy of Division of Armed Forces History
Smithsonian Institution, Washington, D.C.

The Americans sent out patrols in the hope of drawing some of the British forces into disruptive engagements. There were skirmishes, but no significant encounters, since the British wanted to concentrate on establishing their siege lines. Their battery began a steady cannonade of the fort on 7 August. Improvements to the American lines were slowed but not stopped by the shelling. In the southern part of their camp, beyond reach of the bombardment, work on Towson's battery continued unimpeded until it was finished on 10 August.

The British soon concluded that their first battery was too far back to be effective. They began work on a second one further inland, about 200 yards from the river and 750 yards from the fort. Their work parties were even more exposed to artillery fire, and the American gunners strafed them with explosive shot, inflicting high casualties. Nevertheless, the British established a defensive line anchored by the two batteries that was 1,000 yards long and came within 450 yards of the U.S. positions at its closest point.

There was a constant toll in dead and wounded as the two sides sniped and sparred. As the lines solidified, the potential cost of victory in human lives soared. Even for those American soldiers who would escape death or injury in battle there was the danger of illness. Whitehorne found certificates of disability issued after the war that listed rheumatism, hernias, and haemorrhoids as common complaints of survivors, unpleasant results of their physical exertions in building up their defences. Williamson was pleased to hear this, for it complemented the results that continued to flow in from osteobiographical analysis. Owsley's team of physical anthropologists in Washington was reporting multiple signs of physical stress in the skeletal remains.

One odd feature shared by many of the skeletons was lesions in the spine, which could well have resulted from heavy lifting and other physical strain. The human spine consists of vertebrae linked by discs. These discs are composed of an outer ring of tough cartilage surrounding an elastic inner tissue. Along with their attached ligaments, the discs absorb

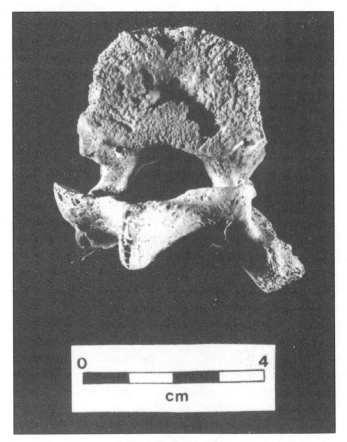

Schmorl's depression.

vertical pressure while preserving mobility of the spine. When overloaded, however, they will rupture, leaking inner tissue out of its cartilage shell. The herniated material may then put pressure on adjacent parts of the spine. If it is forced back towards the spinal cord it can cause nerve damage and pain; if it moves forward or to the side, it will eventually calcify and form bone spurs. If it goes up or down, it wears against and eventually erodes adjacent vertebrae, causing minute indentations called Schmorl's depressions. This usually happens slowly as small quantities of disc tissue are squeezed out, but as the emissions calcify their abrasive effects increase. This syndrome is most common in the middle of the back, the area of greatest biomechanical strain.

Thirteen of the twenty-seven skeletons that the physical anthropologists examined exhibited Schmorl's depressions. Many had lots of them. One had them in eleven affected vertebrae, another nine, and six skeletons had five or more. This unusually high incidence could be explained by the physical strain endured by the American soldiers at Fort Erie. Habitual lifting and twisting of heavy loads could easily have caused such damage. Would the soldiers have noticed the wear and tear? Their backs would have become slightly less resilient as some of the discs lost their cushioning properties, but none suffered damage severe enough to cause serious back problems.

Osteobiographical analysis generated still more evidence of hard labour. Most of the skeletons suffered from other spinal conditions that could have been the result of excessive physical strain. They also exhibited lesions in the bone where muscles had been pulled, healed, and torn again. Some were apparent where chest and shoulder muscles attached to the rib cage and upper arm. These muscles could have been strained by an action such as shovelling. About 60 percent of the skeletons displayed similar marks in their legs and other bones where major muscles attached. Such lesions generally result from prolonged muscular stress rather than a single incident of overexertion.

For the archaeologists this was all good news. The arts and sciences combined were producing vivid insights into the experience of the Snake Hill soldiers in the last few months of their lives. It was an exciting first harvest of interdisciplinary effort. At the same time, Whitehorne's research continued to throw light on historical generalizations about the War of 1812. He was discovering ample evidence that however ill-organized the American army had been earlier in the war, it had developed a sophisticated system of logistical support by the time it began its Niagara operations in 1814. He was able to reconstruct an almost day-by-day account of the American army's occupation of Fort Erie from quartermasters' records.

The quartermasters in the American army of 1814 were expected to account scrupulously for the government funds they dispensed. This made them notorious penny-pinchers, but superb record-keepers. Since they were the ones who had to pay the bills, their papers provided a daily record of the support systems of the army. Their ledgers covered the purchasing of supplies, requisitioning of equipment, contracting of labour, rental of facilities – every commercial relationship necessary for the support of an army in the field.

Without a well-developed supply system, a large-scale military operation like the one at Fort Erie would have been impossible. Immense efforts were required to keep the men fed and the weapons firing, as well as to ensure that the wounded were cared for and evacuated. The

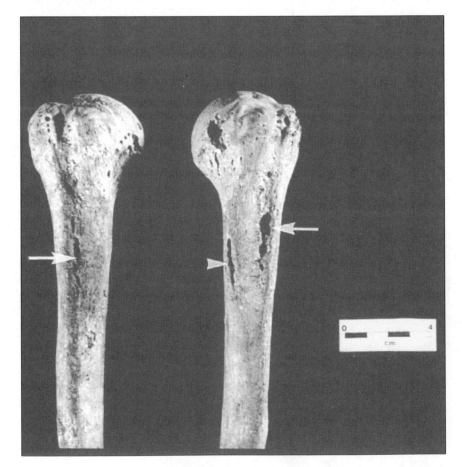

Lesions in the upper arm bones.

THE OX

The ox was buried about sixteen metres northeast of the nearest military graves. It lay on its left side, with its back against the south wall in the deepest part of the pit and its legs angled upward into the shallower portion of the shaft. The head and neck were stretched forward as if the carcass had been dragged by the neck or horns to the grave.

Damage to the ox's ribs, legs, and shoulders suggested that it had been killed by an explosion below its belly. The detonation of an explosive shell would have caused injuries of the sort displayed by the ox's bones. No trace of the right front leg was found. Nor was there any evidence that the beast had been butchered for meat after its death. The only artifact associated with the skeleton was a small piece of iron, approximately seventeen millimetres long, which resembled a section of bent nail. It lay just inside the rear of the rib cage.

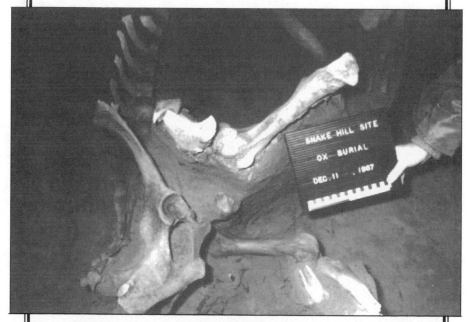

Right hind leg of ox shows dislocation from pelvis and damage to lower left leg.

The ox appeared to have been a neutered male that was at least ten years old and probably nearing the end of its useful working life. Perhaps malnutrition had caused the bones to appear older than they really were. The presence of an old animal, however, was consistent with military records, which indicated that by early fall army purchasing agents had difficulty obtaining healthy young oxen. Frontier farmers would have been reluctant to sell draft animals – their means of production – just when the war had brought a huge market to their doorstep. The poor quality of the beast did not reflect corrupt or incompetent purchasing practices, but the drain that the war was placing on local resources.

The ox was significantly smaller than modern cattle. Larger, improved breeds were beginning to be exported from Britain to North America, but it is possible that they had not yet reached the Niagara region.

No military artifacts were found with its remains, but such equipment would have been removed before the animal was disposed of. Although there was no absolute proof that the ox was an American military draft amimal, this was the reasonable conclusion to draw. The injuries it displayed suggested a death from artillery fire, and its grave was located a respectful distance from, but still near, the human cemetery.

construction effort at Fort Erie added greatly to these standard logistical problems. One thing these records illustrated vividly was the massive scale of the American defensive preparations. Records showed that there were 220 horses in the camp for hauling materials and other duties. Orders were placed for 400 shovels and 200 axes at a time. Military engineers kept demanding tools and supplies throughout the summer. In the first week of September, for instance, plans for an assault on the British lines prompted a request for 610 broadaxes "without delay." A junior quartermaster officer was engaged full time at Fort Erie just to keep track of the materials being sent across the river from Buffalo. At least the American supply lines were relatively secure; the passage across the mouth of the Niagara River was protected by their naval control of Lake Erie. The Americans lost two ships to a daring British raid on 12 August, but this had little effect on the general movement of goods and men between Buffalo and the fort. Several small boats regularly plied the crossing, most often under cover of darkness to avoid British fire.

This facet of Whitehorne's research explained the presence of the ox skeleton at the Snake Hill site. The quartermaster's papers recorded the procurement of eight yoke of oxen in early August. They were put to work pulling heavy materials between the dock and the fort and between the fort and the outer works. Oxen were plodding compared to horses, but they could pull far heavier loads for longer periods of time. Efficient beasts, they ate less than their equine competition. Still, an army inspector reported in late September that the oxen at Fort Erie were suffering from malnutrition, neglect, and overwork. The oxen were never groomed, they could not graze, they were fed too much hay and too little grain, and their food was simply dumped on the ground where it got mixed with foreign materials, including waste. The poor animals also suffered from pulling heavy loads that were poorly balanced.

On top of all this, they were no more immune to the British bombardment than human defenders. Later in the summer, more oxen were brought over to supplement existing teams and replace casualties. They were probably stabled by the docks not far from Snake Hill, so it was not surprising that one of their dead would be buried adjacent to the nearby human cemetery.

The climax of the siege of Fort Erie was the British night attack of 15 August. A number of factors prompted General Drummond to hazard an all-out assault on the American positions. The U.S. fleet that Brown had been expecting a month before finally arrived off the mouth of the Niagara River on 4 August, threatening the British line of supply along Lake Ontario. This led Drummond to consider means of bringing the confrontation to a head. Then, on 14 August, a British shell happened to strike a small American ammunition magazine, blowing it sky-high with a tremendous explosion. Drummond thought that the Americans had been badly hurt and demoralized by this blow, and that a quick attack would catch them while they were still reeling.

In fact, the damage caused by the explosion had been relatively minor. Drummond also miscalculated on other fronts. He estimated that there were about 1,500 defenders left at Fort Erie, when in fact there were 2,800. But his biggest mistake was to plan a three-pronged, converging night attack that would depend on co-ordinated timing for maximum effectiveness. This approach required his troops to make their way in the dark across rough, unfamiliar terrain – through woods, bogs, gullies, and streams – while maintaining a tight schedule. It was a recipe for disaster. Drummond had also ordered his troops to remove the flints from their muskets to avoid an accidental discharge that would betray their surprise attack. They were expected to advance stealthily and dispatch the defenders by bayonet while the bulk of the American army slumbered.

This last order was particularly disastrous, because the Americans were expecting the attack. They thought that the British might try to exploit the apparent advantage they had gained from the magazine explosion that day. As one American officer recalled, "The British thought to surprise us, as they did our troops at Fort Niagara ... but we were ready for them by God, we were ready; a full third of the garrison on duty and the rest of us sleeping by our guns with the dark lanterns lit and the linstocks ready and the cannon charged so full of grapeshot you could reach in the muzzle and touch the last wad by hand." When the bombardment from the British guns slackened towards midnight, and then stopped entirely, the American command put its entire army on full alert. All the batteries were fully manned and most of the American infantry waited with muskets loaded, eyes straining to discern any sign of movement in the night shadows.

The first British attack came at Towson's battery on Snake Hill. At around two o'clock in the morning, the American pickets on the slope below the battery heard the enemy advancing. Before all the sentries could withdraw behind their lines, a force of 1,300 British regulars and Swiss mercenaries charged towards the battery. They ran into devastating fire from above. The six six-pound guns of the Towson battery and the muskets of four infantry companies blazed away as they charged up the slope. Not only did the British lack any element of surprise, they could not return the fire because they had no flints in their guns. Under the circumstances their charge was truly heroic, surging to within a few feet of the American line before breaking on the abattis in front of the ditch. Four more times in the next half-hour the British made the same suicidal rush at the American positions, and each time they were raked by musket fire and grapeshot and forced to fall back. In desperation some of the British soldiers tried to wade out into the river to get around the abattis and the American lines, but some defenders heard their splashing, opened fire, and cut them down in the water.

It was a slaughter. The British finally quit the field, leaving corpses hanging in the abattis and wounded men drowning in the river. As for the Americans, one participant recalled, "By the time it was all over, the Second Artillery was just exhausted – we dropped beside our guns, every muscle aching from the chore of loading, firing, loading again. At daybreak, we could see the bodies piled high in front of our guns. Corpses floated down the Niagara for hours."

The Snake Hill attack was supposed to be coordinated with simultaneous assaults at other points along the American line, but the southern part of the battle was over before any other British columns made contact. The assault on Douglass's battery began half an hour later. Once again it was the British rather than the Americans who were surprised, and despite two determined assaults the attackers were blown back by withering fire from the American guns. The British attack lost any semblance of order as both enlisted men and officers were shredded by grapeshot at close range.

A third British force attacked the main fort. It encountered the same fierce resistance, but on its third assault some attackers managed to scurry up scaling ladders and get a toehold on the parapet of the northeast redoubt. Reinforcements scrambled in behind them, and in desperate fighting the British managed to capture the bastion. The Americans turned the guns of the nearby Douglass battery on the British position, but the attackers held on, repulsing two counterattacks and securing their position as dawn broke over the battle scene.

Then, just as it seemed as if the British might triumph, the magazine beneath their feet erupted skyward with a tremendous explosion. Bits of men and debris were hurled everywhere. An American officer who watched nearby recalled the incident:

Every sound was hushed by the sense of an unnatural tremor, beneath our feet, like the first heave of an earthquake, and almost at the same instant the centre of the bastion burst up, with a terrific explosion, and a jet of flame mingled with fragments of timber, earth, stone and bodies of men rose to the height of one or two hundred feet in the air and fell in a shower of ruins, to a great distance all around.

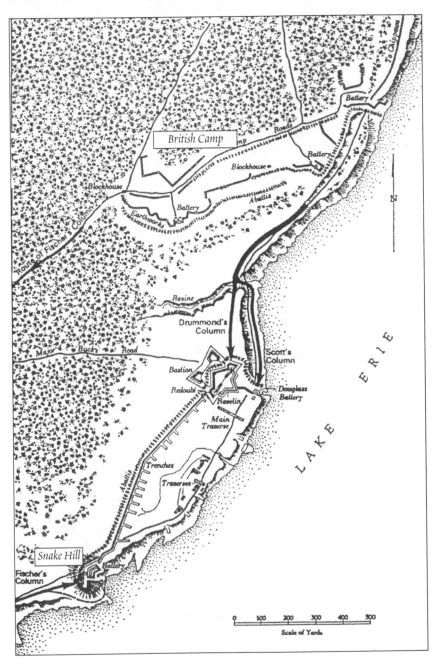

The British attack on 15 August 1814.
Based on **The Pictorial Field-Book of the War of 1812** by Benson J. Lossing
(New York: Harper & Brothers, 1868).

Suddenly, the battle was over. The catastrophe had completely shattered the British position, killing or wounding nearly 400 men and dazing hundreds of others. Many of the British survivors were captured; the rest withdrew as best they could.

The night of 15 August had been a disaster for the British. They had suffered at least 1,000 casualties, more than ten times as many as the American defenders. Part of this lop-sided result was attributable to the unlucky explosion at the fort, but it was also a result of sending men with unloaded guns against fortified positions manned by alert defenders. The slaughter at Fort Erie that night foreshadowed the staggering escalation of warfare in the century to come. From the modern perspective, the British attack through the abattis against the overwhelming fire of entrenched defenders at Snake Hill is reminiscent of nothing so much as First World War assaults through barbed wire into machine-gun fire.

For the archaeological team investigating the Snake Hill skeletons, however, the important question was whether their subjects were casualties of the battle of 15 August. Many of the buttons they had found in the graves came from American infantry and artillery regiments that had defended Towson's battery. But that did not prove that the men were Americans who had died that night. The failure of the British attack meant that the siege would drag on until the approach of winter. There were many more eventful weeks ahead, and many different facets of the American operations would have to be investigated before this central question could even tentatively be answered.

But there were encouraging signs that the Snake Hill mystery could be solved. The initial results of collaborative historical and scientific research had been impressive. The confidence and enthusiasm of the researchers mounted as they found their conclusions reinforced by parallel avenues of inquiry. For physical anthropologists, it was a rare treat to have their scientific tests confirmed by historical documentation. For a historian like Whitehorne, it was amazing to see hard physical evidence that supported conclusions drawn from musty old papers found in government depositories. The archives and the laboratory were working together in a productive partnership.

Chapter 4

STEPS TO THE GRAVE

The hundreds of British soldiers killed at Snake Hill on the night of 15 August fell near where the military cemetery was discovered 173 years later. But they were not buried there. Too many died that night to allow for neat burials; instead, their remains were heaped fifty at a time into trenches dug by American work parties. The bodies of about two hundred British soldiers who were shot in the lake or along the shoreline were allowed to float away down the river. On the other side of the American encampment, hundreds of corpses and dismembered body parts were dragged off the northeast bastion of the fort as quickly as possible so that the damage caused by the explosion could be repaired. It took two days to pass them over the embankment in front of the Douglass battery and bury them with honours in mass graves.

Fortunately for the British wounded, the American field medical system was up and running at the time of their night attack. It took several hours to get all the injured, many of them badly burnt, out of the ruins left from the explosion. They were treated in regimental field hospitals in the camp and then transported to army hospitals across the river. Some suffered from such severe powder burns that it took four days for them to recuperate enough to be evacuated.

Were the American defenders who died that night buried in the graveyard near Snake Hill? Probably not. The more evidence Whitehorne uncovered, the more probable it seemed that the Snake Hill burials were soldiers who survived the British attack only to fall victim to disease, bombardment, or skirmishing in the months that followed. Their fate was all the more poignant because they had survived the worst bloodshed of the summer of 1814 only to be killed with just a few weeks remaining in the campaign.

Their last few weeks of life were probably even harder to bear than the gruelling training and campaigning that had come before. The old expression that an army marches on its stomach is true as far as it goes, but it does not go far enough. An army camps on its stomach as well, and the American army's sojourn at Fort Erie was no picnic. It was essential that the troops be fed to maintain their fighting strength; it was also a logistical challenge that became increasingly difficult as the summer wore on.

In civilian life the soldiers had probably eaten a lot of salted meat and unprocessed corn meal, supplemented occasionally by potatoes, butter, milk, vegetables, and fruit. Rural fare was particularly monotonous because local products were limited, transportation of fresh meat and produce was poor, and food preservation was rudimentary. The soldiers' daily rations were a bit more varied, including salt pork, hard bread, a few vegetables, molasses, salt, vinegar, and a quantity of rum, whisky, or brandy. This was hardly an attractive diet by modern standards, but at least it was more dependable than civilian diets – as long as the army supply system was functioning smoothly.

Whitehorne's study of the quartermasters' records showed that it had not taken long for the 2,800-man army to drain the Buffalo area of most of its excess food supplies. Spirits, salt, and vegetables were often scarce, and the quartermasters always had a difficult time laying their hands on vinegar and soap. Since there was only one small storehouse in the fort, many foods had to be kept in open storage, where they often spoiled. Periods of bad weather increased this wastage and also made it difficult to ship fresh produce across the river.

Most of the soldiers had their own messes where they cooked their meals. In several cases, however, the quartermaster hired local women or the wives of soldiers to cook for a group of men, especially for fatigue parties or groups of teamsters and carpenters who were working hard but not part of an organized larger group like the regular infantry. As the siege continued, salt meat and hard bread were the only foods that the soldiers could really count on. These were not enough to maintain their health and energy, let alone their morale. When mealtime was one of the few things to look forward to in a seemingly endless routine of hard and dangerous work, yet another serving of rancid-looking salt pork and hardtack could be a bit disappointing. Stories of soldiers griping about army food are a cliché today, but in 1814 the Americans at Fort Erie had good reason to protest – and they did so in almost every letter home.

Their officers were not indifferent to these complaints; indeed, they were truly concerned that their troops were eating so poorly at a time when they were working very hard. The shortage of fresh vegetables was particularly worrisome because of the risk of scurvy in the ranks. After the British attack in mid-August, General Brown allowed civilians to come across the river to sell produce, hoping the free market could provide what his supply system could not. Thereafter the soldiers could buy butter, onions, potatoes, and even prepared foods like pies or cooked meats from these local entrepreneurs. But the prices were grossly inflated – not only was the risk of crossing the river factored in, but demand always outstripped supply. So many soldiers continued to eat a monotonous diet low in essential nutrients. Things got so bad that on 25 August the commanding general instructed the chief quartermaster to procure potatoes at any price "to save my men from the ravages of sickness which is making rapid approaches toward paralysing my strength."

Whenever Whitehorne discovered new and useful information of this kind he would immediately telephone Williamson, who could then compare the news with the results of the scientific tests on the bones. Williamson was pleased to see that the physical evidence of poor diet again complemented the historical record. In their examination of the skeletons, Douglas Owsley and Robert Mann of the Smithsonian and Sean Murphy of the National Museum of Health and Medicine found clear evidence of malnutrition. Extreme and prolonged nutritional deprivation leads to the formation of small pits in the bone of the skull, and almost a quarter of the skulls from the Snake Hill burials displayed mild cases of this surface porosity. The consequences of not eating enough vegetables were still etched in the bones of the Snake Hill victims 173 years after their deaths.

There was also extensive evidence of the soldiers' general diet in the condition of their teeth. The dental health of the victims was studied by two other American physical anthropologists, Paul Sledzick of the National Museum of Health and Medicine and Peer Moore-Jansen of the University of Tennessee. They discovered one good effect of the monotonous menus of the era: they inhibited tooth decay. The teeth of the skeletons were generally free of cavities, suggesting a lifetime of eating a diet low in carbohydrates, sugars, and other foods that cause bad teeth. Later in the nineteenth century the molasses and unprocessed corn meal staples of this era would be replaced by highly processed foods such as granulated sugar and refined white flour, which would ensure that subsequent generations of Americans would have much poorer teeth.

The general dental health of the Snake Hill skeletons not only surpassed that of succeeding generations, it was surprisingly superior to that of most of their contemporaries as well. Physical anthropologists had data on comparable groups which suggested that the Snake Hill soldiers had more and better teeth than might have been expected for people of their place and time. Here again, a comparison of the archival and biological evidence offered an explanation. The soldiers' relatively good dental health was probably a reflection of the army's recruiting process. The conscription laws of the day allowed wealthier men – who would have had a richer diet and consequently worse teeth – to avoid serving in the army. Moreover, although there was no direct evidence of dental health being a criterion for enlistment during the War of 1812, there was documentary evidence from later in the century that the army explicitly sought recruits with good teeth. This may have been true in 1812 as well. Strong teeth were desirable not just for general health reasons, but because they were required to tear open the paper cartridges containing shot and powder during the loading and firing of a musket. Indeed, some of the skeletons' incisors showed signs of wear that might well have been a result of this practice.

Studying the skeletons' teeth also provided some insights into the unique characteristics of different soldiers. One man's teeth, for instance, showed evidence of pipe-stem wear. Another had a jaw that projected abnormally beyond his teeth. This condition, caused by an abnormally crowded dentition rather than an unusually large jaw, is known as "Hapsburg Jaw" because it is the product of a recessive genetic trait first noticed in inbred European royal families. Its presence did not mean that there was a Hapsburg prince in disguise serving in the American army; this soldier's condition probably resulted from excessive inbreeding in an isolated rural community.

Despite the good general condition of their teeth, the soldiers were not entirely free of dental problems. Their diet may have been salutary, but the theory and practice of dental hygiene and safety were primitive at the time. Some showed signs of having suffered from abscesses, impacted teeth, and other painful dental maladies. Toothaches from these afflictions must have added to the long list of burdens borne by the soldiers during the campaign. At least they were likely to get better dental care in the army than they would have received in civilian life. Although dental intervention was primitive, it would have been possible to have a tooth pulled

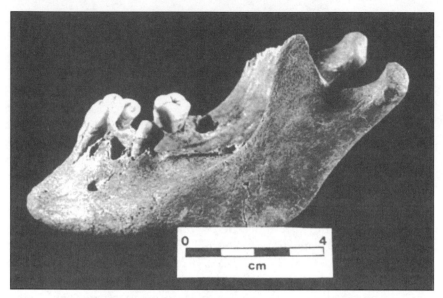

"Hapsburg Jaw," probably resulting from excessive inbreeding.

or a cavity filled. Indeed, although the skeletons had low levels of tooth decay, they often had one or two teeth missing, which suggested that the general solution to a toothache was to pull out the offending tooth.

Toothaches were probably the least of the health problems that plagued the soldiers. Far more dangerous was the risk of serious illness. Contagious diseases were deadly in the days before inoculations and antibiotics. Armies, which brought masses of humanity together at close quarters, multiplied the danger of contagion and were particularly prone to epidemics. During the American Revolutionary War, it was estimated that up to 95 percent of all military deaths were from disease. By the early nineteenth century, medical care had improved enough to reduce this figure to about 75 percent. Still, military campaigns were more likely to founder in sickness than in strife.

Many outbreaks of illness sprang from unsanitary conditions, which few medical experts of the day associated with disease. Doctors knew a fair amount about how the body was put together and how its major parts worked, but they were entirely ignorant about micro-organisms and the mischief they could wreak. Indeed, conventional wisdom made some assumptions about the interplay of environment and health that were completely wrongheaded. One notorious example of contemporary sanitary practice was found in the British army, where a collective tub was used instead of individual chamber pots to collect "night soil" in the barracks, then emptied and filled with water for morning libations. It was not until the 1840s that a connection was made between this practice and a high incidence of eye infection in the ranks and a two-tub system introduced. Another misconception was that dampness was a cause of disease. People rarely washed themselves or their living quarters because they were afraid of getting sick. Since there wasn't room in the Fort Erie barracks for 2,800 men, most of the American soldiers were housed in tents. (All the canvas that could be found in the Buffalo area was requisitioned for this purpose, and large quantities of planking were sent over for flooring.) At first these new quarters were relatively free of infection, but in time they developed into teeming incubators of bacteria.

General Winfield Scott was far ahead of his time in his ideas about sanitation and health. When the men were in training the previous spring, he had required them to bathe three times a week. Moreover, they were instructed to do so in the lake rather than the creek, so they wouldn't end up drinking their wash water. Scott also required tents to be struck and aired out on the first fair day after every rain, and he made sure that his men's food was of good quality by ordering his officers to inspect it before every meal. Evidently Old Fuss and Feathers' nickname was well earned.

Scott's measures were effective in improving the health of the troops. When they had first arrived that spring, doctors had reported cases of pneumonia, disabling rheumatism, cholera, typhus, syphilis, smallpox, dysentery, and various unknown forms of fever and diarrhoea. At first some of these outbreaks verged on epidemics, but by early summer the army's general health was much improved. It remained good as long as their environment was relatively stable, even resisting new infections such as the typhus reintroduced by reinforcements in late June.

During the course of the campaign, many soldiers complained of occasional attacks of rheumatism, which their doctors attributed to their prolonged exposure to the elements. The problem got worse during the siege of Fort Erie when they put in long hours working out of doors; bad enough, in fact, to debilitate some of the men. But the physical anthropologists could find few indications of serious cases of rheumatism or arthritis in the Snake Hill skeletons. There were mild cases in just four individuals, and only one who showed signs of it in more than one joint.

The soldiers were more susceptible to various ailments by late in the summer because both their strength and their clothing were wearing thin. The longer the soldiers spent toiling and fighting in Canada, the more their equipment and uniforms deteriorated. By the end of August, over a hundred men in one rifle regiment lacked shoes, and the rest of the army was not much better off. Back-up stocks of uniforms had been absorbed by reinforcements who had arrived over the summer. Things would only get worse in the months ahead. The freshly outfitted army that had marched out the previous spring was reduced to a motley crew of barefoot wretches, their once-proud uniforms worn and ragged.

Indeed, by the end of the summer, Scott's rules of hygiene were almost completely forgotten under the stress of battle conditions. Camp sanitation was poor at best, with open latrines and waste pits found near campsites and mess areas. Personal cleanliness was left almost entirely to the individual soldier, who had other concerns that seemed more immediately relevant to his survival. The combination of stress, poor diet, crowding, unsanitary conditions and inadequate clothing made the American soldiers at Fort Erie easy prey for infectious diseases.

Soon the army surgeons were reporting a wide variety of cases of intestinal infections and fevers among the troops. Their diagnoses were not always exact or reliable; they often simply matched the symptoms they saw to general patterns of well-known types of diseases. Cholera, for instance, was a common diagnosis. Although this was "common cholera," not the deadly Asiatic strain that would come to North American in the 1830s, it was still life-threatening. It was transmitted by microbes that found their way into the gut through contaminated water or food. Soldiers who were stricken by it suffered from violent diarrhoea and vomiting. Numerous cases of dysentery were reported as well. It was contracted the same way and caused similar symptoms, but was called the "bloody flux" because of the blood-stained, watery mucus passed in its advanced stages. Often these afflictions were fatal because the victim would become so dehydrated that his vital organs would shut down. Those who had mild cases and were able to replace their fluid losses still suffered from piles and hernias caused by the continual stress the diarrhoea imposed on their intestinal tracts. In many instances these side effects alone were debilitating.

Typhus was another common disease reported by the army surgeons. Its presence wasn't surprising: it was contracted from micro-organisms in lice or flea faeces that would pass into the bloodstream as the infested soldier scratched away at his skin. The first symptoms were headache, coughing, constipation and chills. A rapidly rising fever would set in, prostrating the victim, then in four or five days a rash would break out over his entire body. The fever would only break after two weeks of suffering. In some cases, however, toxins generated by the bacteria would poison the blood, causing the patient to become delirious, fall into a coma, and die of heart failure.

Since the army surgeons were not expert at distinguishing between different types of diseases, they tended to lump a host of other related sicknesses together as "fevers." One group of fevers they did single out was what they called the "ague," malaria-type illnesses caused by parasitic microbes transmitted by mosquito bites. These parasites would feed on red blood cells until they ruptured, releasing more parasites into the bloodstream, a process that subjected the victim to a two-day cycle of shivering and chills succeeded by a raging fever, which would in turn be followed by sweating copious enough to drench bedding. Sometimes the parasitic infestation blocked blood vessels in vital organs, with fatal results.

Sick soldiers got more medical care than they would have in civilian life, but it was questionable whether this attention was better for their health. The army surgeons generally had far more sick than injured patients in their care, yet they had no idea of how to cure them. A common treatment for most illnesses was to rid the body of the disease by inducing vomiting and prescribing laxatives. This was effective for the cases of food poisoning that were not uncommon in the Fort Erie camp, but for other afflictions it did more harm than good. If this "puking and purging," as it was called, did not work, blood-letting was the next step. This treatment seems colossally stupid from the modern perspective, but the surgeons were operating on the ancient theory that health was a reflection of the balance of the "humours," components of the blood. Sickness indicated an imbalance, and judicious bleeding was believed to restore the bodies' humours to their proper levels. Leeches were sometimes used to do the job. The result, of course, was that many patients were severely weakened by the treatment and succumbed from the combination of the illness and the cure.

Opium or alcohol were the only drugs available to lessen pain. Otherwise drug therapy was crude, and mostly misguided. One of the few effective remedies was quinine (known then as Peruvian or Jesuit's bark), which helped alleviate malarial symptoms. Calomel, a mercury preparation, was used to treat dysentery, often in doses large enough to make the gums bleed. Like acetite of lead (prescribed for the same purpose), or artrite of ammonia (a diarrhoea cure), it could cause death if taken in large enough quantities, and many patients probably died of overdoses.

An army at war is similar to any large industrial operation that ships in raw materials and ships out a finished product. Food and equipment come in, and sick, wounded, and dead soldiers go out. To deal with medical problems the American army had to have a medical support and evacuation system every bit as elaborate as its supply organization. Whitehorne discovered that the Niagara campaign of 1814 stretched the American army's medical systems to the limit. Shortages of medical supplies were as much a problem as shortages of food. As military patients overwhelmed civilian medical facilities, the army had to build and expand its own hospitals. Sick or wounded men from Fort Erie were shipped across the river, then carried by litter a few hundred yards to a military hospital in Sandytown. By early August the Sandytown hospital was overflowing with 1,100 patients. It was also vulnerable to enemy attack, so as many patients as possible were transferred to a new 350-bed hospital that was opened that month at Williamsville, a village a few miles away.

In addition to these large hospitals on home territory, there were temporary field hospitals behind the lines at Fort Erie. The 21st Infantry had a field hospital set up in tents in the middle of the army encampment, and the 23rd Infantry had one near Snake Hill. A third was established in September to provide care for the 1,500 New York militia in the camp. Records indicate that it was located west of Snake Hill and worked closely with the hospital there. The militia had separate hospitals because they were maintained by their state governments rather than the federal government. Militia surgeons often worked closely with the regular army doctors, but their facilities and supplies had to be kept distinct for accounting purposes.

Each regiment had its own surgeon and two surgeon's mates. The mates were chosen for their brawn rather than their brains. They had to move bodies, living or dead, and hold writhing patients still during unanaesthetized operations. Whitehorne was able to use quartermasters' records of rations drawn for the 23rd Infantry hospital near Snake Hill to estimate that in August about two hundred men and five women were associated with it as staff or patients. The women served as hospital matrons, performed a variety of thankless and distasteful chores, and were no doubt expected to provide some feminine compassion for the sick and wounded as well. Their pay vouchers show that they stayed at their jobs throughout the siege no matter how dangerous the conditions.

The quality of the surgeons varied tremendously because often the army couldn't be too picky if it wanted someone for the job. Some army surgeons had learned their trade as apprentices, and they were a far different class of medical practitioner from the university-trained physicians. The more conscientious among them were aware that they were not very well prepared for their work. Little progress had been made in American military medicine since the Revolutionary War. Indeed, surgeons who had gained rare combat experience in the earlier conflict had failed to pass on their hard-earned lessons. Now their successors had to learn all over again, on their own, how to deal with the diseases and injuries that were common in wartime.

THE THREE LADS

In one large grave the archaeologists uncovered three bodies: Burials number 7, 12, and 13. This trio came to be known around the dig as "Three Lads." Burial number 7 was approximately thirty-seven years of age, old for a regular soldier, and about five feet eight inches (172.5 cm) tall. He had been buried in the south of the grave on the side closest to the lake. He was probably put in before the others, because his left elbow was overlapped by the right elbow of the skeleton beside him. His skeleton was in rough shape: the facial bones at the front of the skull were missing, including the nasal bones; his collarbone and shoulderblades were damaged; and his hipbones and his pubic bones were fragmented. His left arm was broken and his right arm had been badly disturbed after burial.

More buttons were found with this skeleton than any other, but they were poorly preserved. At least one, however, was from the 15th Regiment of Infantry. Whether or not this was the soldier's correct regimental affiliation, he seems to have been an infantryman. The horizontal positioning of cuff buttons in the grave suggested he had been wearing a double-breasted coatee, the type used in American uniforms before 1814. It seemed that he was also wearing a shirt, vest, and overalls. There were so many buttons, in fact, that the archaeologists believed he might have been buried with another garment used as a wound dressing.

Burial 12, the middle of the three skeletons, had been an unusually tall young man – over six foot one (186.2 cm), and about twenty-two years old. His left leg had been amputated at the hip. Copper pins found around the pelvis suggested the presence of bandages in that area. The pattern of buttons suggested that he was buried without pants on and that another garment had been folded or wadded up to dress his leg wound. His burial at Snake Hill meant that he had probably not lived very long after the amputation.

His skeleton was also in poor condition. Much of his upper face was missing. His collar bone was intact, but his shoulderblades and upper arms were damaged, as were his forearms.

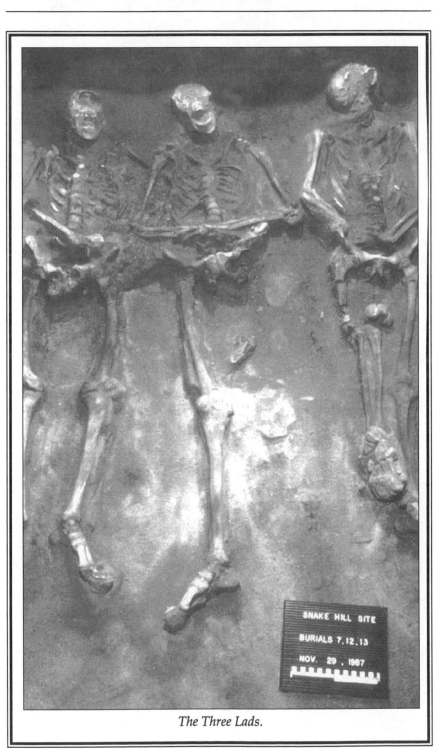

The Three Lads.

Both ends of his right thigh and the lower right leg were damaged. A Y-shaped musket tool was recovered from the right pocket area. It was different from the standard T-shaped American tool and was probably British issue. This did not necessarily mean the soldier was British, however, as it could easily have been an enemy tool that was picked up and pressed into service by the soldier before his death. A feather primer was also found in the grave, suggesting that this soldier was associated with the artillery.

The third of the three lads had been about five foot eight (173.3 cm) and thirty-four years old. He seemed to have sustained massive breakage of his right upper leg; indeed, parts of the leg bone were missing. There was also some damage to the right side of his skull above the ear, to his shoulder blades, his upper right arm, and his pelvis. The left thigh was also broken, but this would appear to have resulted from disturbance after death. A green stain one-third of the way up his left forearm was likely related to a copper cuff link, decorated with a floral design. Although it was a civilian cuff link, he had also been wearing a military garment of some kind, either a coatee or a roundabout. It had been severely damaged, however, and was missing too many buttons to be identifiable. The presence of buttons from a civilian shirt suggested that the victim might have belonged to a militia unit. It was unlikely that he was buried wearing overalls; they had probably been removed to facilitate medical examination of his injured right leg.

Whitehorne found pertinent information about the army's medical support systems in quartermasters' records and the writings of Dr. Amasa Trowbridge, a surgeon with the 21st Infantry at Fort Erie who had left personal papers and memoirs relating his wartime experiences. But to understand how Trowbridge and his contemporaries would have treated their patients, he had to turn to experts in medical history. Adrianne Noe, a medical historian at the National Museum of Health and Medicine of the Armed Forces Institute of Pathology, pieced together a picture of the state of medicine at the time from a variety of sources. This was a particularly exciting project for a medical historian. It was always possible to read documentary accounts of diseases, injuries, and their treatments, but the Snake Hill skeletons offered a rare opportunity to also see tangible evidence of the results of these procedures.

One of the most dramatic features of the Snake Hill skeletons was the evidence they displayed of battle wounds and treatments. Thirteen of the soldiers had broken bones that looked like projectile injuries. Seven had fractured thighs, two had fractured skulls, three had broken forearms (one had both broken), and there were broken ribs and shoulder bones as well. Altogether the physical anthropologists found fifty-three fractured bones among twenty-six complete skeletons. The Snake Hill graveyard was a vivid testament to violent injury and death in wartime.

Most of the injuries appeared to come from shells, shrapnel, and cannonballs rather than small arms fire. This probably reflected the fact that the British bombardment continued to be as heavy following the attack of 15 August attack as it had been before. Indeed, the thirty days after the attack were remembered by the Americans as being the hardest of the whole siege. Between two and five hundred rounds of artillery fire rained down every twenty-four hours, killing or wounding about half a dozen men a day. The British fired on any target visible or suspected, including the American work parties that were burying British dead. On one of the worst days, 27 August, there were more than twenty American casualties from the bombardment.

Most of the incoming projectiles were solid shot, but they included explosive shells and rockets as well. There was no escaping it. One British mortar shot fell directly down a chimney into the officers' quarters, where it ricocheted around the kitchen, killed one of the cooks, then dropped into the basement. Another cannon shot obliterated the pillow of an officer who had just raised himself off his tent bed to reach for a pitcher of water. The cannonballs came in at a low trajectory, often hitting the ground and skipping, ripping through rows of tents and whatever else was in the way. The physical danger was very real; the resulting psychological

stress all-pervasive. Some soldiers hid their fear by mocking British marks-
manship or racing the cannonballs as they rolled through the camp-
grounds. Others couldn't take the stress, and deserted as soon as they saw
an opportunity.

Night brought no respite; the bombardment continued around the
clock. In a postwar letter, an American army corporal recalled being hit by
a British cannonball:

> Just at twilight as my arms were extended in the act of lifting a
> vessel on the fire, a 24 pounder came booming over the ramparts
> and struck off both my arms above the elbows! The blow struck
> me so numb that at first I could not see. My left arm, as I was
> subsequently informed, was carried from my body some two rods
> and struck a man in his back with such force as nearly brought
> him to the ground. This same shot took off the right arm of
> another soldier standing not far from me, and passing on to the
> other side of the encampment, killed three men!

The media following the dig were very interested in this sensational
account, especially when it was reported that two amputated arms that
appeared to be from one individual had been recovered from one of the
medical waste pits. But the forearms unearthed at Snake Hill were severed
below the elbow and did not match those described in this anecdote.

Another bizarre incident recorded during the bombardment was the
"razor's-edge" death of 27 August. A sergeant was well behind the lines
getting a shave from his corporal when a British eighteen-pound cannon
ball ricocheted off the battlements and took off his head and the corporal's
hand. This anecdote also caught the imagination of the twentieth-century
press. It created an overnight sensation when someone noticed that one of
the Snake Hill graves contained a skeleton with no head and that an extra
hand had been found under another skeleton. Two and two quickly
became five: Buffalo newspapers breathlessly reported that the decapitated
sergeant's remains had been found. It was a great story, but Williamson
had to spoil it by announcing that the skeleton had lost his head because
the archaeologists had removed it. "Our headless man died of other
wounds – he had been shot," Williamson said. "We feel very confident in
saying that's not the individual."[1] The presence of the hand in other grave
signified little – there had been plenty of detached hands lying around at
the time. This one had been amputated, and it was unlikely that there
would have been much of the barber's hand left to bury after it was hit by
a cannonball.

But the story of the closer-than-close shave did not end there. In response to the publicity, some Buffalo residents came forward claiming to be the descendants of the headless NCO. "The way it looks to me, he was my great-great-great-grandfather," Robert E. Matthews of West Seneca told a reporter.[2] Apparently Matthews was descended from one of the four young children the sergeant had left behind. He added that there were stories that his ancestor had had a premonition of his death and had told his colleagues in arms that he would never again see his home state of Vermont. Given the conditions behind the American lines during the siege, however, this foreshadowing more likely reflected a pessimist's evaluation of the odds than any supernatural insight.

Although the archaeologists could not claim to have found the headless sergeant, there were other equally dramatic injuries evident among the Snake Hill dead. One of the soldiers had been hit just below the rib cage by a six-pound cannon ball. The shot went right through him, causing an impact so severe that it broke both his legs and hips. Another soldier's skeleton had a brick fragment resting in its spinal column, suggesting that he had been hit by debris from a cannonball hitting a wall or an explosion. Yet another had died from a musket shot that hit him square in the forehead – at least, that was what the physical evidence suggested. His skull was shattered above the eyes and musket shot was found resting inside it. Interestingly, it was only the American army that used musket shot of this type. It was quite possible that this soldier had survived a skirmish with the British only to be mistaken for an enemy and shot by one of his comrades as he returned to his lines.

This case was a reminder that there was still combat throughout the late summer and early fall of 1814. Almost every day there were skirmishes between the two forces, some of them quite hard fought. The most dramatic encounter of this period came in mid-September. On 4 September, the British completed a third battery that was only 500 yards from the U.S. positions. It contained three twenty-four-pound cannons, an eight-inch howitzer, and a mortar. This arsenal represented an upgrade in artillery power that would substantially escalate the damage to the American lines. To counter the threat and steal some of the initiative from the British, the American command decided to stage a raid on the second and third British batteries.

Almost 4,000 militia had been raised in northern New York during the late summer. They became known as Porter's Brigade, after Brigadier General Porter, the officer responsible for the successful call-up. Some of these militia reinforcements were brought across from Buffalo under cover of darkness on the night of 9 September. They set up a rude camp just west of Snake Hill. On 13 September, the Americans increased their artillery fire on the British positions and mounted more patrols to gather intelligence and cover "pioneers" who were breaking trails towards the west flank of the British lines. On the morning of 17 September the artillery fire was stepped up another notch. Around noon two columns of American attackers set out towards the two British batteries under the cover of blustery, rainy weather. They approached the British undetected and took the defenders of the two batteries by surprise. There was fierce fighting, but the Americans managed to destroy the two enemy gun emplacements and even occupy the third before the British counterattacked and drove them back to the fort. The U.S. forces sustained over 500 casualties and the British around 700, not including 400 prisoners the Americans were able to take back with them.

In the wake of engagements like this, the army surgeon's work was overwhelmingly macabre. In addition to the ill patients in his care, the hospital would be overwhelmed with maimed and dying soldiers. At these times the surgeon's best ally was speed. He would move quickly from one patient to the next, abandoning the mortally wounded to die, leaving those without life-threatening injuries to mend, and operating on those for whom it might make a difference. Blood and gore would accumulate on his clothes until he looked like a butcher in a slaughterhouse. Following Lundy's Lane, the surgeon for the British 89th Regiment of Foot found himself caring for 220 men with all manner of gunshot wounds. His recollection of the ordeal paints a grotesque scene:

> I never underwent such fatigue ... The weather was intensely hot, the flies were in myriads, and lighting on the wounds, deposited their eggs, so that maggots were bred in a few hours, producing dreadful irritation, so that long before I could go round dressing the patients, it was necessary to begin again; and as I had no assistant but my sergeant, our toil was incessant.[3]

He had no time to rest, and eventually fell asleep on his feet on the third day after the battle. On the American side things were somewhat better because there were wives and other camp followers to help care for the men.

In those days the shot that was used for everything from cannons to muskets was relatively large, and made of metal that was quite soft compared to modern military projectiles. Instead of piercing bodies and leaving neat holes, it tended to spread a bit on impact, splattering flesh and shattering bone. Surgeons were often faced with appalling injuries that they could do nothing about.

BURIALS 20 AND 21

These two skeletons shared the same grave, with number 21 lying closest to the lake. Burial 20 had been about twenty-three years old and five feet ten inches (177.2 cm) tall. His skull displayed clear evidence that he had been shot in the face. The bones around his upper nose were either missing or badly fragmented, and musket shot was found loose inside his skull. He had probably died quickly. Not surprisingly, his feet were not bound, as they might have been if he had been hospitalized. This soldier's ribs had also been damaged. The pattern of buttons found in his grave suggested that he had been wearing trousers or overalls, most likely military overalls that had several buttons missing. He was probably buried in what he was wearing at the time he was shot, and the absence of evidence of a uniform top suggests that he was in a work party or off duty when he was killed.

His neighbour, Burial 21, was about seventeen years old and six feet (182.5 cm) tall. His skull had suffered considerable damage, but the rest of his skeleton was in good condition. Fragments of cloth and metal were discovered near his left shoulder – a buckle, scraps of fabric, little fragments of spring and a cone-shaped piece of copper. Although they were in a location where an epaulette might have been expected, these bits and pieces of metal and cloth suggested that there had been something else there – it was impossible to tell what.

His feet and ankles appeared to have been bound, and copper pins that might have been bandage fasteners were found around his hips. The pattern of buttons was confusing, suggesting that an old garment of some sort had been used to dress a wound. Although there was no evidence in the bones of a mortal injury, the apparent lack of overalls, the binding of the legs and feet, and the presence of bandage pins suggests that he had received medical attention in a field hospital before his death. However, the location of buttons showed that he had still been wearing parts of a uniform and that he was buried wearing a jacket of some type, suggesting that death had come quickly and that he had been hospitalized only briefly. He was like burials 1 and 4, and his companion in the grave, Burial 20, in that the carbon and nitrogen isotope values of his bones reflected a diet high in fish and corn similar to that of prehistoric Iroquoians in the northeast. However, the oxygen isotope values suggested European origins.

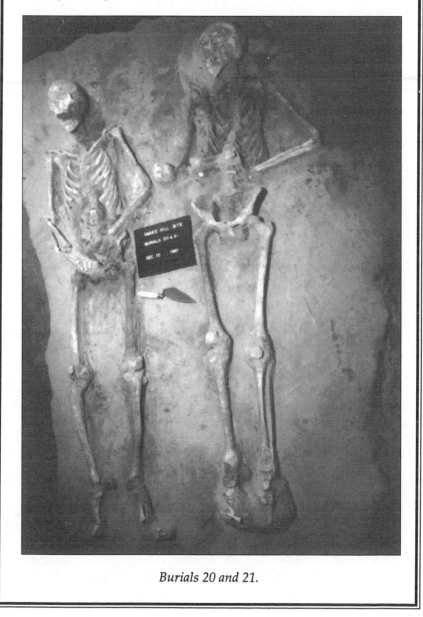

Burials 20 and 21.

Wounds in the chest or stomach were practically a sentence of death. Surgery was not very sophisticated, and sorting out and repairing scrambled guts and organs was simply beyond the capacity of existing medical techniques and technology. But even for those who might have been stitched back together there was little hope of survival because of the inevitability of infection. Dirty hands, fetid bandages, or shreds of soiled clothing mixed in with the torn flesh were just a few of many possible sources of germs. Doctors did not know about antiseptic techniques, but they did know that operating usually made things worse. As a result, they rarely probed body wounds beyond the depth of a finger and did not open up the chest cavity unless they had no choice. Usually all they could do was leave bad enough alone and hope that things would get better. Odds were that they would not. There were no antibiotics. Gangrene or some other ugly infection would set in, and the victim would die a lingering and feverish death from his festering wound.

For injuries to other parts of the body, the surgeons employed a limited repertoire of dubious techniques. After probing around to inspect the damage, they would usually drain any areas that seemed to be under pressure from fluid build-ups. This included trepanning – the technical term for drilling holes into the skull. They would also stitch up simple flesh wounds. Many of the tools they used – levers, knives, scalpels, saws, and forceps – would not have been out of place in a mechanic's tool box.

Although little could be done about wounds to the head, chest and stomach, flesh wounds and injured appendages were a different matter. One of the Snake Hill burials seemed to have been recovering from a wound to his shoulder. When bone is damaged from infection or injury, new bone is produced at the site of trauma. This soldier's right shoulder appeared to have been mending for a little more than a month. Perhaps he survived his first wound, returned to duty, and was injured again, this time mortally. But this was not necessarily a surgical success story. It is also possible that he was too sick to be moved from the field hospital and died a lingering death from infection a few weeks after his initial injury.

Amputation was the most common operation performed by early-nineteenth-century army surgeons because it was the one type of surgical intervention at their disposal that clearly improved the patient's chances of survival. It dealt with the limitations of contemporary trauma care by avoiding them. Lopping off limbs was a sure way of transforming ragged and complex wounds into relatively simple ones and reducing the risk of infection at the same time.

Although it was a horrible procedure for the injured patient to endure, it was thought that a healthy man had a better chance of

BURIAL 15

This twenty-one-year-old six-footer (183.7 cm) was tall for his time. Height was not necessarily an advantage during a siege. A copper pin, with fibres of fabric and hair stuck on it was found on the left side of his skull, suggesting that it had been bandaged. The inside of the skull displayed lesions that also pointed to the presence of a head injury. The presence of new bone formation in his right shoulder suggested that it had been injured four to six weeks before his death. It is also possible that he had been in the field hospital, too sick to move, for a month or more before succumbing to infection or disease. It is also possible, but less likely, that he had recovered from his shoulder injury and returned to duty when he sustained a mortal head wound. Damage to his bones had not stopped with his death: his entire left side had been badly disturbed in the grave.

Burial 15 skull and bandage pin.

surviving the shock of amputation than the drawn-out agony of transportation to a far-off hospital and an extended convalescence. In many cases, proper care could have saved the limb, but proper care was out of the question because the surgeons were so busy. Amputation was the best use of the limited time they had to give a patient. Most of a regimental surgeon's job in the wake of battle was to assess the damage and risk of infection to legs and arms, then saw off as many limbs as necessary as quickly as possible. The speed with which the surgeon could dismember his patients during these times of crisis was considered the true test of his abilities. William Dunlop, surgeon to a British regiment of 1,000 men, reported that he sawed off nearly 200 limbs after the Battle of Chippawa.

Despite their many limitations, the army surgeons' knowledge of the mechanics of the body was quite good and the amputation techniques they employed were basically the same as those used today. The patient would be given a shot of whisky or a couple of grains of opium to numb the pain. If neither of these was available, he would simply be given a musket ball to clamp between his teeth. To limit bleeding, a tourniquet was wrapped tightly around the leg or arm just above where it was to be cut off. Then a surgeon's mate grasped the man's leg with both hands and held it steady. The surgeon first made an incision through the skin and underlying tissue, pulling them aside to reveal the muscle underneath. Then, with a steady and firm stroke of the knife, he quickly cut through the muscles and tendons to the bone. At this point blood from the veins and arteries would gush out in a torrent from below the wound. This often unnerved inexperienced bone-cutters, but veterans knew that the tourniquet still stemmed most of the life-threatening flow from above. Next an assistant used a retracting device to pull the muscles back away from the incision while the surgeon cut them away from the bone. When there was room enough for a saw blade, the actual cutting began. The bone had to be sawn off quickly before the patient bled to death. In a few seconds a strong-armed surgeon could cut almost all the way through. A little tug would snap the last bit of bone and finally sever the limb. The surgeon would tie up arteries and wash away the clotted blood with warm water, then fold the leftover flaps of flesh, skin and muscle into a blunt stump and fasten them in place with adhesive plaster. An accomplished practitioner could finish the whole bloody job in under a minute. If the patient was lucky, he would pass out from the pain and not swallow the musket ball.

Despite the agony of this ordeal, 40 to 60 percent of amputees survived. A captured British private who was transported across to Buffalo before his amputation recalled the procedure as "tedious" and was coherent enough afterwards to get angry at an orderly for casually tossing his severed hand onto a nearby dung heap. Within a couple of days he was gambling and drinking rum. However, for every such remarkable recovery there were those who succumbed to blood loss, shock or subsequent infection.

The medical waste pits that the archaeologists discovered at Snake Hill contained clear evidence that there had been a close connection between the graveyard and one or more of the nearby field hospitals. Eight surgically amputated limbs were recovered from these pits. In one the archaeologists found bones from a right arm and a left arm that might have come from the same individual. Another disgorged a complete left leg with a foot attached, cut off near the top of the thigh and fractured in its lower thigh bone. All of these amputated limbs displayed clean saw marks and a little tab of bone at the end of the cut where they had been snapped off. Not all the limbs found there had been cut off, however: a left forearm was found that displayed no saw marks and may have been blown off.

The medical waste pits and the amputated limbs suggested that the graveyard had been a burial ground for the hospital nearby. There were

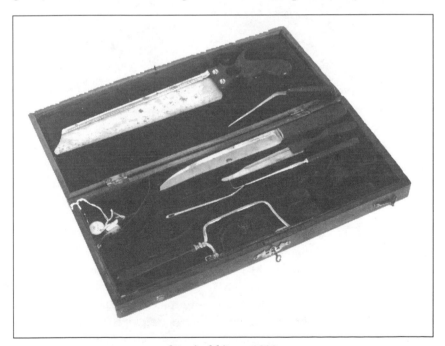

Surgical kit ca. 1800.
Courtesy Canadian Parks Service.

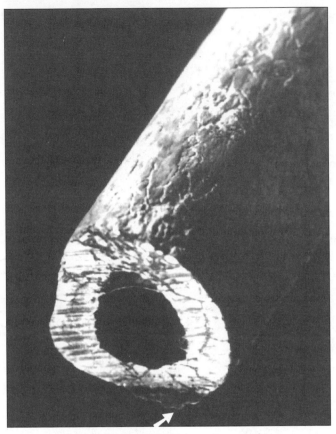

Surgical amputation – see snap mark.

references in American military records to a small graveyard that was described as being "just back of Towson's Battery." Although half of the Snake Hill skeletons showed signs of traumatic injuries or amputations, the other half displayed no evidence of how they had died. This was not surprising. Serious abdominal wounds, or minor wounds that led to lethal infections, would not have left any trace in the skeletal frame. Many of the diseases that plagued the American soldiers killed their victims by causing a rapid dehydration that would have not been apparent in the skeleton either.

There were no torn, blood-soaked uniforms to provide any additional clues: they had long since rotted away. The archaeologists found only the occasional tiny scrap of cloth remnant from soldiers' uniforms. In a few cases, copper salts from corroding metal buttons had stopped bacteria growth and preserved some of the wool.

Still, there was a related, if slim, basis for speculating about cause of death in each case. The pattern of buttons in each grave suggested how each soldier had been dressed when he was buried. This in turn provided grounds for guessing how he had died. A soldier who was killed instantly would probably have been buried wearing his full uniform. Those who had been hospitalized for a long time would have had most of their uniforms removed. In between these extremes the state of dress suggested the degree of treatment received by the victim. The wounded who took a while to die would probably have had their uniforms unbuttoned to ease their breathing, or portions of clothes removed to facilitate access to their injuries.

The buttons found in the graves suggested that two of the Snake Hill burials had been clad only in shirts with bone buttons. They may have been longer-term hospital patients, or they may have been killed while sleeping. In some of the other burials it appeared that the soldiers' military overalls had been removed. In two of these cases, the men had obviously suffered injuries to their lower legs; another may have been injured in the pelvic area. Sometimes the overalls seemed to have been opened, perhaps to allow medical treatment of abdominal or upper leg wounds.

There was corollary evidence of hospitalization in some cases. A few of the graves contained straight pins that were probably used to fasten bandages. In other instances, the distribution of buttons suggested that

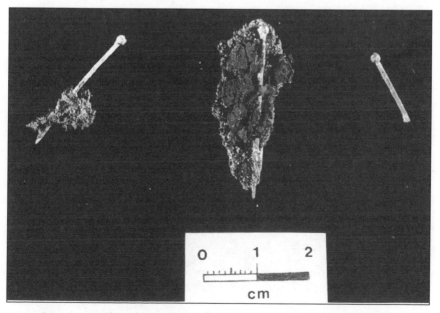

Copper pins found near injured areas on a number of the skeletons.

parts of military garments had been used as bandages for the chest and stomach. Sometimes, too, the positioning of the knees and ankles of the skeletons indicated that they had been bound together before burial to make it easier to carry the corpse. This was a practice that would likely have been part of preparation for burial after death in a field hospital rather than a practice for burying men killed while on duty.

The Snake Hill graves did not appear to have been dug at the same time according to a symmetrical plan. Although all the graves were arranged in rows, some were better aligned than others. Many of the graveshafts showed signs of having been dug in haste. Some were so narrow that their occupants had to be squeezed into them; in others more than one body shared the same grave. This was understandable for burials performed under the hazards of battle conditions. Yet some were so ample and well-proportioned that they seemed to have been prepared during relatively calm periods in the siege when there was time to pay attention to such niceties. Nails and fragments of wood found in some of the graves showed that a few of the victims had been buried in coffins, while others had not. All of this suggested that the burials had come at different times under differing circumstances. This would have been consistent with a trickle of dead from a nearby field hospital rather than the fallout of a battle in which hundreds were killed. In the latter case, death on a mass scale

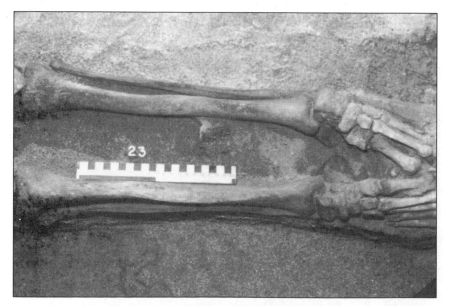

Positioning of the legs and feet of Burial 23
indicates that they were bound.

meant that corpses were denied any individual importance or special burial treatment.

The theory that the Snake Hill cemetery had served a field hospital explained both the presence of an American military graveyard and its small size. The Snake Hill skeletons were probably those of soldiers who had died instantly of their wounds or were so seriously sick or wounded they could not be evacuated to American territory. Since the number of soldiers buried at Snake Hill represented just a fraction of the American casualties during the fall of 1814, the limited number of burials at Snake Hill suggests that in general the American medical evacuation system was working and that most of the sick and injured soldiers were removed to American hospitals for recovery.

The few who had been left behind, however, provided eloquent testimony of the trials endured by all of their companions in the campaign of 1814. Theirs was not a glamorous war, if ever there was such a thing. At Fort Erie they found only hard work, malnutrition, disease, and the constant threat of violent death from cannon shot, musket ball or bayonet. If they were sick or injured enough to need hospitalization, a whole new series of tortures awaited them. Lucky indeed was the man who returned from the war no worse for wear and wiser for the experience. For those who were buried on the Canadian shore, death may well have come as an equally blessed release.

Chapter 5

PROOF OF CITIZENSHIP

After the American sortie in mid-September, the confrontation at Fort Erie settled into a stalemate. Both sides were suffering from sickness and low morale, and neither felt capable of dislodging the other. The British commanders took a hard look at their situation: ammunition was running low, and an outbreak of typhus in the ranks threatened to swell into an epidemic. They decided to pull out. The British began moving their heavy equipment and stores back to the Chippawa River on 18 September, the day following the sortie. On the 21st, their infantry left its campfires burning and trudged back to Chippawa. The siege of Fort Erie was over.

The American campaign had a few last sputters in it. A new army division had arrived to reinforce the Fort Erie garrison, and finding its original mission unnecessary, decided to challenge the British at Chippawa. The 4,500-man force landed north of Fort Erie on 8 October and immediately advanced towards the enemy. On the 15th there was an artillery duel between the two forces, followed by skirmishing over the next few days. But the Americans decided that the British positions were too strong, and withdrew to Fort Erie on 21 October.

Meanwhile, the survivors of General Brown's original army were finally returning home. Brown's men left Fort Erie for good on 20 October, and Porter's militia withdrew and was demobilized at around the same time. The last medical facility at Fort Erie, the militia hospital, closed on the 19th after sending all its sick and wounded to Buffalo. The new American occupants of the fort made tentative plans to stay the winter, then changed their minds, fearing that the severity of the weather would make their position untenable. The men and boats necessary to evacuate troops and equipment were assembled, and the withdrawal commenced. On 5 November, the last few units of American troops set explosive charges around key emplacements of the fort, got into their boats, and rowed away as Fort Erie erupted in smoke, dust, and flying rubble behind them. The Niagara campaign of 1814 was over.

So was the war. The Treaty of Ghent was signed on Christmas Eve, ending hostilities. No significant territory had changed hands. In fact, no significant concessions were made by either side. The Americans had probably held on to Fort Erie as long as they did in the hope that it at least would provide a bargaining chip during peace negotiations. Ironically, transatlantic communications were so slow that the peace negotiators never knew that it had been given up. But it made little difference. Despite triumphant claims on both sides, the war had achieved nothing. Like the siege of Fort Erie itself, it petered out in an indecisive anticlimax that made the carnage and suffering it had caused all the more tragic.

The futility of the sacrifice made by the Snake Hill soldiers did not change the fact that they had fought and died in the service of their country. The discovery of their remains provided an opportunity to acknowledge their sacrifice 173 years later. In March of 1988, representatives of Fort Erie, Buffalo, and the armed forces of both Canada and the United States met at the Garrison Inn in Fort Erie to conclude plans for an appropriate ceremony to repatriate the skeletons. Newspaper, radio, and television reporters from both sides of the border attended the press conference that followed to catch up on a story that had been left dangling since the dig ended the previous fall. Fort Erie alderman Doug Martin, chairman of Fort Erie's repatriation committee, formally announced that all the American soldiers would be returned to their homeland after a ceremony to be held on 30 June during the Fort Erie Friendship Festival.

Dead soldiers are perhaps not the best symbol of international friendship, but holding the ceremony in conjunction with the festival made sense in that the rationale for establishing the event the year before had been the 175th anniversary of the outbreak of the War of 1812. The end of the war might have been a better date for the celebration of cross-border amity, but that would have meant delaying, for another two years, an event that was certain to be an effective tourist attraction for Fort Erie. The festival was inspired by the idea that since the war peace and goodwill had prevailed between the two countries. This assumption was not borne out by history. The peace treaty had settled boundary questions and led to a disarmament treaty on the Great Lakes, but these agreements were necessary because of the hostile relationship that continued between the two countries. For the rest of the century both sides spent millions reinforcing their border defences in the expectation of war.

But details such as these could not stop a good idea. The Friendship Festival, originally intended to be a one-day, one-time celebration, had expanded and endured. The festivities were extended to four days, and the Buffalo Chamber of Commerce had come on board. Other border cities had been invited to embrace the concept. The National Geographic Society was induced to petition Congress and Parliament to declare July 2 and 3, the two days between Canada Day and Independence Day, "U.S.-Canada Days of Peace and Friendship." Although Congress and Parliament declined to do so, the success of the first festival, which pulled in about $1 million in tourist revenue, inspired organizers to make it an annual celebration. The repatriation ceremony promised to make its second coming really special.

There was only one hitch: it had yet to be proved that all of the soldiers were American. Everyone assumed they were, but providing conclusive evidence was a different matter. History could make a convincing circumstantial case, and science could supply important corollary evidence, but the burden of proof rested on archaeology. It was here that the painstaking techniques applied during the dig really paid off. The exhaustive site cataloguing that had revealed and recorded essential physical information about each burial would be vital in positively identifying the soldiers as Americans.

The best clues to nationality were the buttons found in almost every grave. They had become corroded and encrusted after almost two centuries underground, but it was still possible to measure the size and discern the design of some of them. A total of 403 buttons of different types had been found, and each grave had revealed them in different quantities and patterns. It took weeks of work to catalogue all the information about each one – what it looked like, what it was made of, where it was found, and its relationship to nearby buttons. Organizing these data was a task of daunting complexity. ASI archaeologist Stephen Thomas solved the problem by devising a computerized inventory system that compiled details about every button on a data base that could be accessed in a variety of different ways. When finished, it would provide a means of answering different questions about the buttons with statistical profiles of the collection in whole or in part. Planning this system took time and careful fore-thought; implementing it took far more time and data entry throughout the winter and early spring of 1988.

The archaeologists were able to turn to some arcane reference works to guide them in their identification of the buttons that still had discernible markings (see table). By far the most numerous were pewter buttons, about seven-eights of an inch (23 mm) across, inscribed with a stylized "I". This was the basic U.S. infantry uniform button of the day (the "I" stood for infantry). A smaller number of American buttons had an eagle, or the letters "US" emblazoned on them. Two had the much rarer inscription of "RA" (Regiment of Artillery). Although most were pewter, some were copper or brass. Diameter was a significant factor because different parts of the soldiers' uniforms would have had buttons of different sizes. The team was even able to confirm for the first time that the small pewter four-holed button found on many sites of this period was in fact used on American overalls – a discovery of some importance for military historians. American and British buttons were quite different. The British uniform buttons were usually more ornate, with regimental numbers and often some royal emblem engraved on them.

Button Types Discovered
Script "I" 140
Eagle 29
"US" 23
Script "RA" 2
Other American 1
British 5
Civilian (floral).............5
Other 2

Although most of the graves contained enough buttons from American military uniforms to establish nationality, it was very difficult to determine whether the soldier was from the militia or the regular army, and if the latter, his regiment. In theory, it should have been easy to determine the grave of a regular soldier. Historical accounts and illustrations provided the archaeologists with a good idea of what the uniforms of Brown's army had looked like. These uniforms all sported similar buttons. The regulars wore grey wool jackets, known as roundabouts, over a pair of white military overalls. The roundabouts, made of a lighter wool than the regular winter-issue coats, were short-waisted with long sleeves, and had buttons running up their fronts and on their cuffs. The overalls had three

A soldier of Scott's brigade.
Painting by Don Troiani, Southbury, Ct., U.S.A., based on research by James L. Kochan.

BURIAL 4

The only clue to the cause of death of Burial 4 was his fractured lower right thigh. This alone would not have killed him – if it was life-threatening, the leg could have been amputated. But another mortal injury that did not injure any bones may have been sustained at the same time. This soldier was five feet nine inches tall (175.5 cm) and had been in his late twenties or early thirties when he died. Like some of the other soldiers, he had eaten a native diet rich in corn and fish, but his teeth were in such bad shape that they probably bothered him constantly. There were fatigue fractures in his bones that were consistent with marching long distances with a heavy pack or the hard labour of building defensive works.

The hexagonal pattern of nails around his skeleton indicated that he had been buried in a coffin. There was a great deal of wood intermixed with the bones of his feet, which had been badly disturbed and scattered toward the right of the body, perhaps by rodents. He was buried with his arms at his sides, his hands on his thighs, and his body turned slightly to the right.

This soldier seemed to have been wearing an intact uniform, possibly one that was practically new. The buttons found in the grave were in good condition and lay in a pattern consistent with their placement on the regular army uniform. In fact, his grave had one of the most complete button assemblages among the skeletons. It contained round pewter buttons from the soldier's overalls. These had a pattern of four holes, with a depressed centre – a U.S. type. A single row of smaller pewter buttons, round and flat, conformed to the pattern of the American roundabout (short uniform coat). No shirt buttons were found in the grave, but they may have been made of wood and decomposed. The button evidence found with Burial 4 conformed to the uniform of an infantryman in a regular unit more closely than that of any of the other burials.

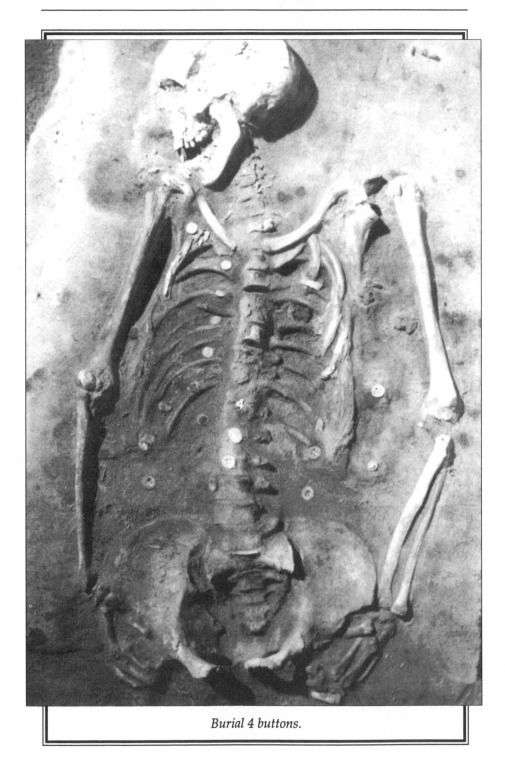

Burial 4 buttons.

flaps fastened by buttons at the chest, and suspenders buttoned to a high waistline. With this information it would seem that all that was necessary to identify the grave of a regular infantry soldier would be to look for infantry buttons lying in a pattern that matched their placement on the soldiers' original uniforms.

But it was not that simple. First of all, the positioning of buttons in the grave was subject to a number of variables. During the campaign, soldiers would have replaced lost buttons with whatever substitutes were at hand, sewing mismatched buttons on with originals. Extra buttons carried in various pockets could also end up in different parts of the grave. Then there were the complications introduced by the possibility that injured soldiers had flaps opened or clothing taken off to facilitate access to wounds or to ease their breathing. In such cases certain buttons would be missing, or would have fallen into unlikely areas. To further complicate matters, pieces of uniform used to bind wounds would have introduced new and different buttons into the grave. It also had to be borne in mind that buttons overlying hard tissue like the rib cage would have remained closer to their original positions as the body decayed than buttons on soft-tissue areas like the abdomen.

It was particularly difficult to make sense of the jumble of buttons often found at the mid-point of the skeletons. Here jacket buttons converged with buttons from coat-tails, pockets, suspender straps, and overalls. Many of the soldiers were buried with their hands folded across their stomachs, adding cuff buttons to the mix. Occasionally the arms were rotated so that these cuff buttons were trapped under the forearms where they were readily identifiable, but this clarified only a small part of the larger mess.

With all of these complicating factors, it was usually impossible to be sure whether a soldier was militia or regular army. Not only was it possible that regulars would have had incomplete uniforms, it was equally likely that the militia would have worn regular army uniforms, or at least parts of them. Some militia units had only civilian clothes, but others had been issued partial or complete uniforms that would have left button patterns exactly like those of regular soldiers. Records that suggested that some had been in older-style uniforms were strongly substantiated by the types and patterns of buttons in two of the graves. Many more graves yielded both civilian and military buttons, suggesting that their occupants had been militia men as well.

The archaeologists were disappointed by the impossibility of clearly identifying regimental affiliation or distinguishing between regulars and militia, especially since early in the dig they had hoped that some of the

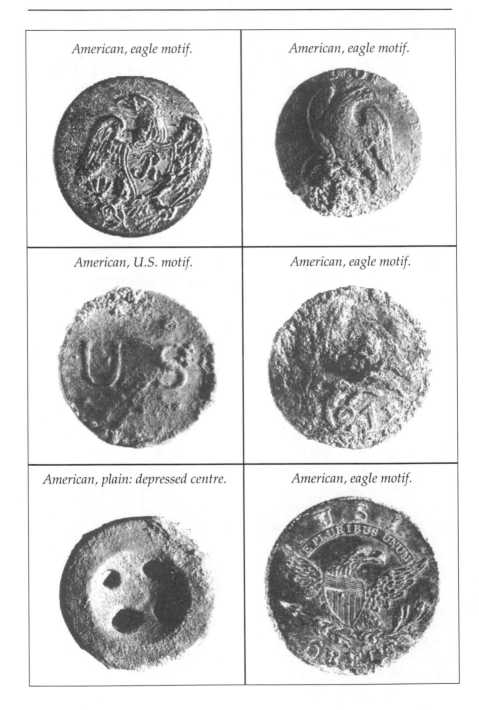

American, eagle motif.

American, eagle motif.

American, U.S. motif.

American, eagle motif.

American, plain: depressed centre.

American, eagle motif.

dead soldiers would eventually be identified by name. There were a variety of ways in which this might have been possible. It was thought that personal effects providing a name or at least strong clues to a soldier's identity might be found in some of the graves. As it turned out, the only artifacts other than buttons found with the soldiers were gun flints, straight pins, the odd musket tool, and a spoon. Whitehorne provided an explanation: army regulations stipulated that all personal effects be removed from the dead before burial and sent to their families. This was the responsibility of first sergeants or adjutants in the field; hospital matrons did the same for those who died under medical care. As a result, there would be no easy shortcuts to identifying the soldiers. As Major Mike Wood pungently put it to a reporter, "You're not finding guys in complete uniforms or uniquely constructed coffins that have a lot of memorabilia with them that says "OK, this is Joe Shmoe and here we are."

Still, it seemed possible that clues to the identity of one of the individuals might be found in historical records. There were many accounts of soldiers' deaths, and perhaps Whitehorne would turn up one that described injuries matching those of one of the skeletons, or at least mentioned the victim's burial at Snake Hill. Some, like the story of the sergeant decapitated while having a shave or the bilateral amputee, superficially matched Snake Hill remains and caused a stir when their similarities were first noted. But ultimately none of the anecdotal evidence

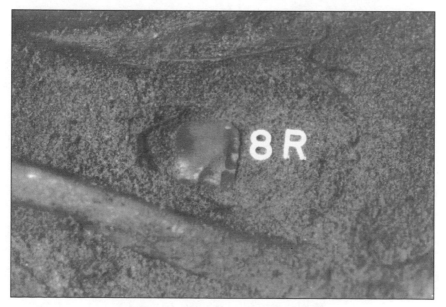

Gunflint found in the pocket of Burial 8.

T-shaped musket tool found in the pocket of Burial 10,
used to keep the musket clear of obstructions.

matched the injuries and physical characteristics of the bones found in the Snake Hill site. Nor were any accounts of a burial at Snake Hill discovered. This was disappointing, but not surprising, considering that the Snake Hill burials represented just a small proportion of the hundreds of Americans who died during the siege. With these odds, such an identification would have been a fluke.

Nevertheless, personal identifications remained a slim possibility. Whitehorne had been able to find the names of the soldiers in service at Fort Erie from muster rolls and pension and bounty requests that were preserved in the archives. The muster rolls noted individual deaths and how many soldiers died at different times. Their precise use of language was helpful: "died" meant death by disease or accident; "killed" indicated an artillery fatality; and "killed in action" signified a man who had fallen in close combat. They also provided various physical details such as height, age, hair colour, and other distinguishing characteristics such as scars.

It seemed plausible that some or all of this information could be cross-referenced with the skeletal evidence to produce a name in at least one or two of the cases. Although they had only the bare bones to go on, physical anthropologists were able to determine the approximate height and age of each victim. Stature could be estimated from the length of

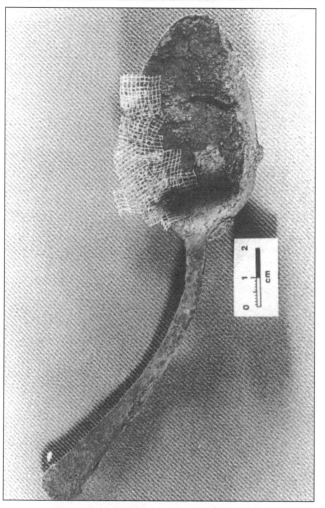

Spoon found in the pocket of Burial 10.

principal bones. Age could be pegged quite precisely for victims who had been adolescents or young adults by studying the stage of development of bones and teeth. The amount of wear on teeth and bone joints also provided a basis for guessing an adult's age, although these conclusions were less exact because the ravages of time and environment varied from one man to another. This osteobiograpical information could then be combined with the archaeological data. Button patterns and the injuries evident in some skeletons offered clues to immediate cause of death or hospitalization, which could be compared with the means of death listed in the muster rolls. The regimental or militia unit affiliation suggested by the buttons in the grave would also help narrow down the search somewhat. If, say, a soldier from the 21st Regiment was listed as "killed" at Fort Erie in pension records, and a skeleton of similar height and age with 21st Regiment buttons was found at Snake Hill displaying injuries that seemed to have been incurred by artillery fire, this would have been enough for a tentative identification.

Unfortunately, things didn't work out that way. First of all, the muster rolls weren't always reliable. Some soldiers were reported dead, then discovered among the men turned over during prisoner exchanges with the British. One sergeant's pension request read: "I know I was listed as killed. But I was captured and later exchanged for a British soldier and returned home."[2] The record of payment of a widow's pension, when it could be found, provided the only conclusive evidence that a soldier had in fact died in the siege. Second, most of the descriptions of soldiers in army records were limited to hair colour, scars, or other physical characteristics that would not be evident in the bones. Finally, and critically, it was possible to establish a tentative regimental affiliation for only two of the burials. In Burial 6, nine buttons were identified as those of a soldier in the 21st Regiment of Infantry. However, not enough skeletal material remained in that grave to project physical characteristics that could be cross-referenced to regimental records. In the case of Burial 7, a 15th Regiment of Infantry button was found. This was hardly enough to provide a positive regimental affiliation. Nevertheless, a search of the records of the 15th Regiment of Infantry failed to produce any record of a dead soldier of the same age and height.

Williamson and Whitehorne tried to come at the problem from the other direction by narrowing down the hundreds of names in army records of soldiers who had died at Fort Erie to those most likely to have been buried at Snake Hill. Some could be eliminated on solid historical grounds: it was known, for example, that officers' remains were always returned to the U.S. for burial. To reduce the list substantially, however, more sweeping and tenuous assumptions had to be made. They began with time of death. If they were correct in believing that the graveyard had served a nearby field hospital, they could safely eliminate all the deaths before August 15 on the grounds that the cemetery would not have been started west of Towson's battery before the American defence lines were established. Nor did its layout seem to reflect a burial *en masse* for those who died during the attack of 15 August. This reduced the list from hundreds of possibilities to dozens. Eliminating soldiers who would have died during the sortie of 17 September cut out dozens more. Finally, they ruled out soldiers from regiments and militia units that would not have served in that area of the encampment. They were left with about sixty names, but there was still too little information for airtight conclusions. The quest for personal identifications of the soldiers had hit a dead end.

Although individual identification proved elusive, the physical anthropologists' analyses of the Snake Hill skeletons generated a lot of descriptive information about both individuals and the group as a whole. Susan Pfeiffer's study of the age of the skeletons at death, for example, produced some provocative results. One of the stray hands found at the site, the one from Burial 5, came from a young adolescent. Pfeiffer estimated that it could have been from a boy as young as twelve. It was against army regulations to recruit soldiers under fourteen, but it was known that drummer boys as young as twelve had been in Brown's army. Still, the thought of even a fourteen-year-old enduring the rigours of the American army's campaign of 1814 was enough to shock modern sensibilities. On the whole, however, it was the maturity rather than the youth of the victims that was surprising. The average estimated age of the group was 21.6 years, and there were more individuals at Snake Hill in their mid-thirties than might have been expected. These scientific conclusions were consistent with the age estimates Whitehorne had compiled from the historical record. Perhaps maturity had been a criterion in army recruitment.

Another notable feature of the Snake Hill group was that it contained proportionately more tall individuals than might have been expected. About thirty percent of the soldiers had been over six feet tall, pushing the average height of the group as a whole close to that of modern men. This was at odds with all other studies of the stature of early nineteenth-century North Americans, which held that in general they were substantially shorter than people today. Clearly the Snake Hill soldiers were not physically representative of their contemporaries. This anomaly may have been attributable to deliberate selection. Recruitment regulations stipulated a minimum height of five feet six inches (168 cm), although this was never effectively enforced. In the case of the Snake Hill sample, however, more rigorous selection criteria may have applied. Whitehorne found evidence that tall men had been specially sought for some army units. Rifle companies, for example, were known to have deliberately recruited taller individuals. He also found a quotation from a captain of one of the Pennsylvania militia companies sent to Snake Hill on 15 September in which he pronounced himself to be only interested in "splendidly big fellows."

In part, the size of the men may have also been attributable to their class and regional origins. Bigger men were found in the most physically demanding occupations in the early 1800s, while people in the country also tended to be bigger than those who were city-bred. Historical research indicated that most of the men who had taken part in the Fort Erie siege came from northern states and that many had been farmers or rural craftsmen in civilian life. This evidence was backed up by the scientists' study of the bones. One of the tests they ran measured the amount of lead in the soldiers' bodies. Lead is not easy for the body to metabolize, so it tends to be retained and stored in the skeleton. Wealthy Americans of the day used lead-lined containers for food storage and preparation and ate with pewter dishes and flatware. Since the lower orders could not afford these items, high lead levels suggested an upper-class background. Alternatively, a silversmith or anyone engaged in a similar occupation in which lead was used on a regular basis would display high levels as well. Lead is poisonous when it accumulates in large enough quantities. Most of the Snake Hill soldiers did not have enough in their systems to cause any problems, but a few had levels sufficient to induce nausea or appetite loss. A couple even had enough to cause occasional episodes of muscle weakness, abdominal colic, or partial nerve paralysis. But on the whole the results of the lead tests were consistent with historical findings: the Snake Hill soldiers were largely a lower-class lot.

The scientists had a battery of other tests to run on the bones as well. One of the most esoteric was the measurement of the oxygen isotopes in the bones as a clue to the place of origin of the soldiers. The same element can have a number of different isotopes depending upon the weight of the atoms that make up its molecules. The isotopes in all natural materials vary slightly in different parts of the world, decreasing with distance from the sea, lower average temperatures, and higher elevation. The oxygen in rain in the Arctic, for example, will have a lower isotope than that in rain in the tropics. The unique oxygen isotopes of a particular area are absorbed in the human body through drinking water and are thus incorporated into the bones. The scientists thought that by measuring the oxygen isotopes in the Snake Hill skeletons they would be able to show that

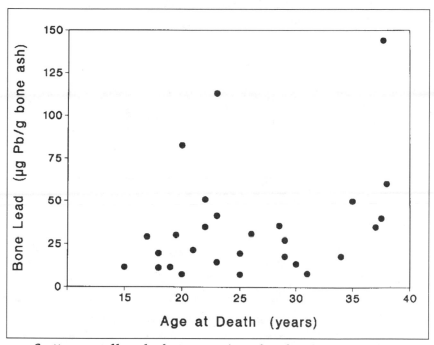

Scattergram of bone lead concentrations plotted against age at death.

the dead men had come from a particular part of North America. It was an approach that had rarely been used before, so they were not sure if it would work. The Snake Hill burials became a test case for this new technique.

The results were promising. The range of isotopes in each individual showed that most had lived their lives in one restricted region. Variations of oxygen isotopes within North America have been mapped, and differences between Ontario and the northern U.S. states allowed for an equation of oxygen isotopes in the bones with citizenship. The Snake Hill skeletons gave readings that might have been expected for inhabitants of eastern New York, Pennsylvania, or most parts of New England. Although there were limited reference samples by which to test these results, their corroboration by historical evidence seemed to confirm their validity.

Carbon and nitrogen isotopes were also measured with the same purpose in mind. The types of carbon and nitrogen found in plants, meat, and fish vary slightly with climate. Humans who have been eating a local diet end up storing carbon with their native isotope in their bones. The carbon isotopes in the Snake Hill skeletons showed more variation between individuals than there had been in the oxygen isotopes. This was

Lead Contact and Poisoning in Barbados						
Organ	Sign or sympton	0–39	40–79	80–119	120–199	Over 200
Intestinal tract	Colic	None	Appetite loss; nausea	Vomiting; constipation; colic	Frequent severe colic	Colic with muscle spasm
Nerves	Palsy	None	None	Weakness in extensor muscles	Marked weakness or paralysis	Extensor muscle paralysis common
Brain	Convulsion	None	None	Occasional	Common	Life-threatening; coma

Note: Individuals vary considerably in the correlation between symptoms and blood levels. This is a function of age and the fact that blood lead levels fluctuate more rapidly than tissue lead concentrations. Values in this table should be viewed as approximations.

Source: Jerome Handler et al., "Slaves: Historical, Chemical and Biological Evidence," *Social Science History* 10 (1986): 399–425; reproduced with the permission of Duke University Press.

General relationship of blood lead level to severity of three symptoms of lead intoxication

not surprising, however, for the local diets in different areas of the United States could vary widely depending on the type of staple foods grown in the area. Some of the soldiers had apparently consumed large quantities of corn and fish, a diet similar to that of North American aboriginals. Most had levels of nitrogen that suggested a diet high in meat and fish. Only two showed evidence of a European-style diet rich in plants unavailable to the average colonial or aboriginal person.

Altogether the archaeological, historical, and scientific evidence presented a picture of a group of young men, tall and robust, who had come from modest rural backgrounds in the northeastern U.S. and endured a number of hardships and dangers before finally dying in the service of their country. Unfortunately, the results of all the scientific tests which would support this portrait were not available to Williamson in the spring of 1988 as he was trying to establish the nationality of the skeletons. The Friendship Festival deadline made definite conclusions necessary by early June.

Williamson was personally satisfied, on the basis of archaeological data, that all of the skeletons were Americans, but to give his conclusions the greatest possible authority he organized a meeting of experts to discuss each burial thoroughly. Joseph Whitehorne, René Chartrand of Parks

Canada, Donald Brown of the Toronto Historical Board, Patrick Wilder of the Sackets Harbor Battlefield State Historical Site in New York, Stephen Thomas of ASI, and Donald Kloster of the Smithsonian met in Toronto for a few days at the end of March to go through all the information that had been gathered. By this point the basic cataloguing of button information was complete. They decided that twenty-two of the twenty-eight soldiers could be positively identified as Americans on the basis of the buttons found in their graves. The rest, they concluded, could be judged as "probably" American on the basis of their archaeological context. The absence of American uniform buttons in some graves was logically explained by the presence of militia at Fort Erie and the existence of field hospitals in the vicinity.

It was not really surprising that no British soldiers were identified. The wartime principle of segregation of the dead would have prohibited the burial of British soldiers in the area. Historical accounts suggested that the British killed in the fighting of 15 August were either thrown into the Niagara River or buried in mass graves elsewhere. After 15 August, when the fighting was focused inland and northward, British soldiers would not have been in the area. Of the five British buttons found on the site, four came from medical waste pits and only one was found in a grave. The buttons in the waste pits no doubt came from body parts that were disposed of without regard for nationality, while the single button discovered in a grave was likely a souvenir from the pocket of an American victim.

Armed with these conclusions, Williamson recommended to the Coroner of Ontario that all of the full skeletons be repatriated. Dr. Ross Bennett concurred, and signed a certificate allowing the U.S. Army to take the bones. At a press conference on June 9, 1988, at the Park Plaza Hotel in Toronto, Williamson announced that the twenty-eight full skeletons discovered at Snake Hill would be repatriated.

It was decided, however, that there was insufficient evidence associated with the partial skeletons discovered at the site to include them with the rest. What would happen to these bones and the bits and pieces found in the waste pits? Scientists on both sides of the border were interested in holding on to some of them.

British 104th New Brunswick Regiment button found in the pocket of Burial 6.

British Royal Artillery button found in a medical waste pit.

Williamson negotiated with a variety of institutions to determine their disposition. Ultimately the collection was transferred to the Museum of the History of Medicine, Academy of Medicine, Toronto; and the National Museum of Health and Medicine at the Armed Forces Institute of Pathology in Washington, D.C. All the artifacts and a few of the amputated bones stayed in Canada. The artifacts were handed over to Old Fort Erie for display. ASI agreed to design and construct a permanent Snake Hill exhibit for the Peace Bridge Authority – to be displayed at the Canadian Niagara Power Building on the Niagara Parkway in Fort Erie – and to display artifacts from the dig during the Friendship Festival.

Not all of the full skeletons were returned to the grave. U.S. legislation allowed pieces of them to be retained for scientific study. Here the different interests of the scientists and the soldiers finally came into conflict. After going to such trouble to retrieve the skeletons, Lieutenant-Colonel Trotter wanted to bury them intact. But Dr. Marc Micozzi of the U.S. National Museum of Health and Medicine was entitled by law to retain pieces of the skeletons for further study. He did so, and the Snake Hill skeletons proceeded to their new graves short a bone or two.

The repatriation ceremony planned for 30 June was modelled on the procedures used when reinterring the remains of American servicemen returned from Vietnam and Beirut. "These boys will be treated as if they were active-duty deaths, as if the young men had died just yesterday," Colonel Trotter explained. "Just because we're late doesn't mean they won't get what they deserve."[3] It was impossible to tell if this is what the dead soldiers themselves would have wanted, but it seemed likely. Whitehorne had come across a number of historical accounts of mortally wounded soldiers requesting burial on the American side of the river. A private in the Pennsylvania militia, for instance, recorded the death of a friend in the following manner:

> Coming to the house at Chippawa, I found Thomas Poe lying on a blanket. He reached his hand to me and told me that he was mortally wounded, that he had but a few moments to live, and told me he wished to be buried on the American side of the river

Tent containing remains, Buffalo skyline in the background –
"so close and yet so far."

... Carrying him nearly a mile across the plain, in the middle of
26 July, appeared to exhaust what little strength he had left. He
shook hands with me for the last time. He said to me in a weak
voice: "Alexander, you will never see me again in this world." He
expired in a few minutes.[4]

Exactly where in their homeland the soldiers would be buried had become
a subject of some dispute. Early media coverage had reported that the
remains would be sent to Arlington National Cemetery, the burial place of
the Unknown Soldier. But cemeteries in the Buffalo area began vying for
the honour of receiving the remains almost from the moment that their
discovery was announced. In Cheektowaga, Councilman Thomas M.
Johnson mounted a campaign to make the local War of 1812 cemetery
the final resting place for the Snake Hill soldiers. The Cheektowaga site
had been the main burial grounds for the nearby Williamsville Hospital,
where most of the sick and wounded of Brown's army had been sent. The
only problem was that there was very little room at the site, which already
contained two hundred American and one hundred British bodies in a
mass grave. The Evergreen Cemetery's "Field of Honour" in nearby Eden
also had its supporters. The question became so controversial that the

Fort Erie's temporary morgue.

American army realized it would be damned for whatever decision it made. Ultimately it decided to rebury the soldiers in a national military cemetery at Bath, New York. "It's a case of federal troops coming to federal land," explained Trotter. Many sites had been considered, but there were two significant factors in the final choice of the Bath cemetery. It was the national military cemetery closest to Snake Hill, and it was located in an area from which many of the men who fought at Fort Erie had been recruited.

As the day of the repatriation ceremony approached, a hockey arena in Fort Erie was converted into a temporary mortuary in which to prepare the skeletons for the ceremony. The soldiers were to be placed in metal caskets according to the same order in which they were discovered. Each skeleton was set on a white sheet atop a green blanket, then the coffins were sealed and draped with an American flag. It sounded simple enough, but in practice it was very difficult to piece all of the skeletons together properly. ASI staff helped make sure that all the right pieces were in the right caskets, and they were kept busy to the last minute arranging the bones in a fashion that was anatomically correct. One final bizarre touch remained. Each soldier received a new set of dog tags before his casket was closed. This was not a sentimental gesture, but rather a means of identifying each burial in case there was a need to disinter them in the future.

On the day before the ceremony, the caskets were moved to Fort Erie, where a Canadian honour guard commenced a twenty-four hour vigil. The repatriation day dawned with grey skies, strong winds, and a chill in the air. Still, hundreds of spectators showed up for the 10 a.m. ceremony.

Guarded, flag-draped caskets at Old Fort Erie.

Organizers had invited Prime Minister Mulroney, Premier Peterson of Ontario, President Reagan, and Governor Cuomo of New York, but had to settle for the American ambassador to Canada, Thomas Niles, the Canadian Minister of Veterans' Affairs, George Hees, Fort Erie Mayor Heinz Hummell and Buffalo Mayor James Griffin. There were also swarms of servicemen from both sides of the border in attendance, some in modern uniform and some in period dress. Redcoats from the Fort Erie Guard and the Fort York Guard manned the ramparts overlooking the grounds outside of the fort where the coffins were lined up. The Fort York Guard had come from Toronto to represent the 8th Regiment of Foot, British troops that had taken part in the siege of Fort Erie. A detachment from the Hamilton Militia District included a guard of honour from the Lincoln and Welland Regiment, a successor of a militia unit that had participated in the siege. The U.S. army was represented by seventy-five members of the 3rd U.S. Infantry, its oldest active-duty infantry unit. Known as the "Old Guard," it was now a special ceremonial unit for the U.S. army. Its members were dressed in Revolutionary War period uniforms and, except for the fife and drum corps, carried muskets with thirteen-inch bayonets.

After the dignitaries arrived and inspected the honour guard, the mayor of Fort Erie addressed the crowd. Then the actual memorial

Spectators watching the American jets fly by – their faces tell all.

service, conducted by Canadian and American chaplains, began. At its conclusion cannon fired in salute and a bugler on the ramparts played the last post. A minute of silence in honour of the dead ensued, followed by another boom of cannonfire and a bugler playing reveille. George Hees said a few words before joining Ambassador Niles in signing documents that made the transfer official. To signify the moment, the Canadian honour guard gave way to American troops, while pipers of the Argyll and Sutherland Highlanders of Hamilton and the Lorne Scots of Brampton played a lament. After Ambassador Niles acknowledged the gratitude of the American government, Canadian soldiers began loading the caskets into twenty-eight waiting hearses while the pipers played "Amazing Grace." With the Old Guard leading and Canadian troops falling in behind, the hearses began to move off towards the Peace Bridge along a route lined by members of the American and Canadian Legions. On the bridge, flags from the War of 1812 – a Union Jack and a Stars and Stripes with fifteen stars and fifteen stripes – flew at half mast. As the cavalcade spread across the span, four American air force jets flew over in "missing man" formation.

All of the members of the project team were deeply touched by the ceremony. As Williamson told a reporter, "It was extremely emotional for my entire staff. To see [the soldiers] treated this way, it's as if they died yesterday."[5] Others in the audience were equally moved. "Their death was the beginning of our peace, a peace we hope will last forever," Mayor Hummell had eulogized.[6] But there were undertones of an ancient rivalry even as peace was being celebrated. In a document distributed to reporters by United States Army representatives, the war was attributed to "the trouble the United States was experiencing with the British during the Napoleonic Wars." This annoyed a Canadian historian, Carl Benn, who took exception to the implication that Britain provoked the invasion. "That was a pretext," he objected, "What really drove this thing was the Americans and their sense of Manifest Destiny. If they'd succeeded, at least Ontario, and perhaps all of Canada, would be part of the United States today."[7]

Reporters in the crowd kept the conflict alive in their quest for good copy. Who won the war? "Everybody knows the Americans won," said ten-year-old Chris Swanson, of Alden, New York, who had attended in the company of his father, a Vietnam War veteran.

"Without their sacrifice we wouldn't have the freedoms we have today," his father added.[8]

On the other side, Bill Stewart, a twenty-one-year-old member of the Lincoln and Wellington militia regiment, took great pride in the role previous members of his unit had played in the historical drama being commemorated. "We might've killed the men we're burying today," he boasted to a reporter with a zeal that was somewhat out of keeping with the general tone of the ceremony. "We proudly defended our border and it's a high tradition we're keeping up today."[9]

This last assertion was debatable, given the numbers of American soldiers in sight. A U.S. army veteran, Richard Mix of Kaylar, Pennsylvania, commented to a journalist as he displayed his ceremonial firearm, "Where else can you cross a border with a rifle and not be accused of starting an invasion?"[10]

Meanwhile the procession of hearses was moving southeast along its 120-mile journey to Bath National Cemetery, where another crowd of hundreds had gathered for the reburial service. Members of the Old Guard carried the casket from the last hearse and placed it by the others at 4:14 p.m. The American flag on the final casket was raised and held up in the face of a brisk wind as a three-volley salute was fired and a lone bugler played taps. Then, as VIPs flew off in army helicopters, onlookers came forward to pay their respects. The Old Guard folded the flags on each of the caskets, and the Snake Hill soldiers were left to be lowered into the earth once more. Each grave would bear a marker that would read simply: *Unknown Soldier, War of 1812.*

*Procession of hearses carrying the remains of the
American soldiers found at Snake Hill. In the lower
photograph, the procession crosses the Peace Bridge.*

THE SNAKE HILL LEGACY

The return of the soldiers to their native ground was a fitting culmination to the Snake Hill project. There was plenty of post-game analysis to come – conference papers, academic articles, more test results, even a book or two – but the repatriation ceremony was the climax and symbolic conclusion to the enterprise. After being disinterred and dismantled, probed and tested, the skeletons suddenly became human again when they were reassembled and prepared for burial. The ceremony had packed a surprising emotional impact because of everything that had been learned about the soldiers' lives and deaths. Many people who had followed the project in the news came to see the soldiers' return and were genuinely moved by the experience. The Snake Hill saga had begun in acrimony, administrative chaos, and financial squabbling, but in the end, as William Fox of the Ontario Ministry of Culture and Communications observed, "Everybody has benefited. It's left people with a really good feeling."[1]

The landowners were happy. Bulldozers had arrived to fill the grave-shafts and restore the original contours of their properties. The Beatties had begun to build a new house in the spring of 1988. On May 16, the U.S. army presented Vincent Dunn and the Beatties with special plaques to thank them for their co-operation, and a few years later they would also be presented with copies of the scholarly book that resulted from the archaeological project. Considering the shock and disruption to their lives caused by the initial discovery, things had turned out quite well. They were applauded by everyone involved for making a personal sacrifice in the interests of the community's heritage. They also ended up with some good stories to tell about the experience. Best of all, when their houses were built and their lives returned to normal, they had the comfort of knowing that they would not be living in the middle of a graveyard.

The Town of Fort Erie was happy. The problems of financing that had worried the town council all along were being resolved. If the free services and salaries of personnel supplied by various institutions were taken into account, the total cost of the project exceeded a quarter of a million dollars. The expenses incurred by ASI after the dig itself ended were eventually covered by other levels of government. The provincial grant of $30,000 in February had been a start. After much foot-dragging, the Department of Veterans' Affairs of the Canadian government coughed up $60,000 in May. The U.S. army was expected to fulfil its commitment to "pay its fair share" by covering the $150,000 the town had laid out for the dig. In the end, Fort Erie came out ahead. It had received an abundance of free publicity that had established it in the public mind as an area rich in history and archaeology. The dig itself had injected money into the local economy, and now that it was over the permanent Snake Hill exhibit enhanced the old fort as a tourist attraction.

The American army was happy. It had made the most of a unique opportunity to demonstrate its commitment to bringing its dead back to U.S. soil. Usually this involved the retrieval of corpses from more recent conflicts where the question of American military involvement was still troublesome and divisive. But in the case of Snake Hill, there were no such drawbacks and some unusual benefits. The repatriation allowed the army to revel in its tradition, to link it with patriotism, and to publicize the connection. Armies know the value of history. A sense of historic *esprit de corps* builds morale, and morale wins battles. Snake Hill was clearly an instance in which the present served the past because the past served the present.

The project team was happy. The ASI staff were relieved to have all the work behind them, but grateful at the same time for a fascinating experience that they would remember as one of the highlights of their careers. Whitehorne had found the project extremely rewarding. As he had conducted his research he had the satisfaction, rare for a historian, of seeing physical evidence emerge to confirm or refine his findings. Conversely, the anthropologists and scientists had been able to study a sample group of bones for which historical information was available to corroborate the accuracy of their theories and techniques. For everyone involved, the Snake Hill project was a professional bonanza that had produced a rich lode of information to draw upon in future work. Soon Williamson and Pfeiffer were putting together a scholarly synthesis that would present all of the historical, archaeological, and biological anthropological research that resulted from the dig in a single book.[2]

Snake Hill had also been a great publicity campaign for archaeology and its related disciplines. People in nearby Ontario and New York learned that archaeology was not restricted to King Tut's tomb in Egypt, but had a contribution to make in their immediate world. The dig was in the news for weeks, reflecting and reinforcing the genuine public interest that followed the discovery of the skeletons. After the dig was over and the soldiers reburied, the interest did not die. PBS produced a short documentary on the subject that aired regularly over the next four years.

Even some of the bureaucrats were happy. The Snake Hill discovery had publicized and promoted the conservation of Ontario's archaeological heritage. For some this only spelled trouble. The Cemeteries Branch of the provincial Ministry of Consumer and Commercial Relations was not overjoyed because the Snake Hill episode focused attention on the need to reform the Cemeteries Act in a way that would only complicate their main job of regulating the cemeteries industry. Snake Hill had a similar effect at the federal level, where an order-in-council had instructed the Department of Veterans' Affairs to add pre-Confederation military burials to its responsibilities in the future. But civil servants working in departments responsible for heritage concerns were ecstatic. Snake Hill had given some of their long-standing concerns a public airing. Out of an initial mess there had emerged a clear public and governmental commitment to the exploration of significant archaeological discoveries.

The Snake Hill project will have long-term importance for the archaeological community if it leads to a heightened public awareness of its concerns and a greater appreciation of their legitimacy in the land development process. The whole saga began with a classic conflict between the opposing interests of economic development and heritage conservation. The rights of private property were pitted against the community's interest in its history and identity. There was legislation in place that tried to reconcile these conflicting ideals, but cases such as Snake Hill showed that it was impossible to frame laws that could anticipate every confrontation that might emerge. Yet Snake Hill also demonstrated that public interest in archaeological discoveries was capable of altering development plans when legal inducements failed. If the best hope for archaeology rests in education rather than legislation, the Snake Hill dig did a lot to advance the cause.

It also demonstrated that archaeological concerns should be addressed long before shovels hit the ground. It is possible to achieve both archaeological and development goals with relatively little friction. When subdivision planning procedures are followed, archaeological assessments can be done well in advance. Potential conflicts can be further minimized by developing archaeological master plans for entire regions. With a year or two of study, archaeologists can flag areas of potential archaeological significance so that municipalities can avoid them when zoning land or approving commercial or residential development. This concept is particularly relevant for an area like Fort Erie. The Snake Hill cemetery was just one of many established in the area during the War of 1812, not to mention the countless other historic and prehistoric sites in the region.

Some Ontario municipalities have already completed master plans that will help them avoid the problems that emerged at Snake Hill. Others are content to deal with archaeological concerns as they emerge with each application for development. Still others, resenting any constraint on development or drain on their tax coffers, ignore archaeological concerns and even violate provincial archaeological regulations.

No doubt there will be other Snake Hills. Some will be hidden from the public and bulldozed into oblivion; others will be discovered and explored. The Snake Hill skeletons have been put to rest, but the problems they brought forth from the grave soldier on.

APPENDIX

Project Team and Researchers

Project Director: Dr. Ronald F. Williamson (ASI)
Administrative Assistant: Mr. Robert MacDonald (ASI)

Archaeology Section:

Ms. Deborah Steiss (ASI)
Ms. Beverly Garner (ASI)
Mr. Andrew Clish (ASI)
Sgt. Lawrence (Jay) Llewellyn (AFIP)
Mr. Stephen C. Thomas (ASI)
Ms. Julie MacDonald (ASI)
Mr. Martin Cooper (ASI)

History Section:

Lt.-Col. Joseph Whitehorne (USA)
Mr. Patrick Wilder (SHB)
Dr. Adrianne Noe (NMHM)
Mr. David Owen (MTR)
Mr. Tim Shaughnessy (NPC)
Dr. Charles G. Roland (MU)

Physical Anthropology Section:

Dr. Susan Pfeiffer (UG)
Dr. Douglas W. Owsley (SI)
Dr. Jerry Cybulski (NMC)
Dr. Shelley R. Saunders (MU/ROM)
Mr. Robert W. Mann (SI)
Dr. Peer H. Moore-Jansen (UT)
Dr. Marc S. Micozzi (NMHM)
Mr. Sean P. Murphy (NMHM)
Mr. Paul S. Sledzik (NMHM)

Artifact Conservation & Identification Section:

Ms. Anne MacLaughlin (ROM)
Ms. Julia Fenn (ROM)
Ms. Charlotte Newton (CCI)
Mr. Stephen Poulin (MCC)
Ms. Sandra Lougheed (MCC)
Mr. René Chartrand (CPS)
Mr. Patrick Wilder (SHB)
Dr. Donald Brown (THB)
Mr. Donald Kloster (SI)

Institution Affiliation Key:

AFIP	=	Armed Forces Institute of Pathology (U.S.)
ASI	=	Archaeological Services Inc.
CCI	=	Canadian Conservation Institute
CPS	=	Canadian Parks Service
MCC	=	Ontario Ministry of Culture and Communications
MTR	=	Ontario Ministry of Tourism and Recreation
MU	=	McMaster University
NMC	=	National Museum of Civilization, National Museums of Canada
NMHM	=	National Museum of Health and Medicine, Armed Forces Institute of Pathology
NPC	=	Niagara Parks Commission
ROM	=	Royal Ontario Museum
SHB	=	Sackets Harbor Battlefield State Historic Site (N.Y.)
SI	=	Smithsonian Institution (U.S.)
THB	=	Toronto Historical Board
UG	=	University of Guelph
USA	=	United States Army
UT	=	University of Tennessee

Dr. Paul Litt was recruited in 1991 to bring the perspective of a Canadian historian to the research and writing of this popular account of the Snake Hill project.

ENDNOTES

EXPLANATORY NOTE:

Most of the information presented in this book is drawn from the scholarly account of the Snake Hill excavation, *Snake Hill: An Investigation of a Military Cemetery from the War of 1812*, edited by Susan Pfeiffer and Ronald F. Williamson (Toronto: Dundurn Press, 1991). These notes refer predominantly to contemporary news reports of the dig.

PROLOGUE

1   Michael Clarkson, "'Snake Hill Skeletons' Homeward Bound," *St. Catharines Standard*, 30 June 1988.
2   Ibid.
3   Michael Clarkson and John Nicol, "An Anonymous Call was the Key to Finding Snake Hill Skeletons," *St. Catharines Standard*, 21 November 1987.

CHAPTER ONE

1   Dana Flavelle, "U.S. Bones from War of 1812 to be Taken Home, Officer Says," *Toronto Star*, November 1987.
2   Patti Lewis, *Niagara Falls Review*,14 November 1987.
3   Robert J. McCarthy and Dave Condren, "1814 Dead Find Last Resting Place," *Buffalo News Graphic*, 1 July 1988.
4   Geoffrey Rowan, "Dead Men Tell Tales," *Buffalo Magazine*, 10 April 1988, 18–22, 27–28.
5   Town of Fort Erie, "Transcript of Archaeological Discovery Meeting," 13 November 1987.
6   At this point Dr. Williamson could only make rough guesses about the potential costs involved. He began by breaking down the project into three phases. The first, field work and exhumation, would cost $35,000 more than had been spent to date; conservation and identification would be another $30,000; and finally, compilation and reporting of results would cost roughly $20,000. These figures were based on the assumption that the twenty-one skeletons discovered so far were all that would be found and that most members of his project team would be paid by their own institutions, as the Americans already on site were. Another $5,000 was added for contingencies. Then there were the town's expenses for security and logistical support. It had already spent $20,000, not counting the administrative costs associated with the diversion of existing equipment and personnel. Added together, these figures totalled $110,000. It would cost another $20,000 to restore the lots to their original condition. That reminded someone that the rental of the Gradall for the next twenty-one days had not been included. It would be $20,000 at most, bringing the project's estimated price to $170,000.

CHAPTER TWO

1   "Fort Erie Landowner Lost His Twin Brother in a NATO Exercise," *Welland Tribune*, 10 March 1988.
2   Craig Sumi, "Bones Excavation an Archaeologist's Dream," *Niagara Falls Review*, Thursday, 14 April 1988.

CHAPTER THREE

1   Eleanor Tait, "Red Tape Mars Archaeological Find," *Hamilton Spectator*, 3 February 1988.

CHAPTER FOUR

1   Mike Vogel, "Tale of War Burial Site Slowly Unfolds," *Buffalo News*, Sunday, 6 December 1987.
2   Mike Vogel, "Headless 1814 Battle Victim May Have Descendants in WNY," *Buffalo News*, Tuesday, 8 March 1988.
3   David Owen, "Local Historian Writes of the Life and Times of a Professional Soldier," *Summer Residents/Friendship Festival*, 28 June 1988.

CHAPTER FIVE

1.   Geoffrey Rowan, "Dead Men Tell Tales," *Buffalo Magazine*, 10 April 1988.
2   Heike Hasenauer, "War of 1812 Graves Found In Canada," *Soldier*, June 1988.
3   Robert J. McCarthy and Dave Condren, "Site Picked for War of 1812 Remains," *Buffalo News*, 14 April 1988.
4   J. Fenton *Journal of the Military Tour by the Pennsylvania Troops and Militia under the Command of Col. James Fenton, to the Frontiers of Pennsylvania and New York*, George Kline, Carlyle, PA, 1814.
5   Eleanor Tait, "Home at Last," *Hamilton Spectator*, 2 July1988.
6   Sarah Sacheli, "War of 1812 Soldiers Return Home with Military Honours," *Fort Erie Times-Review*, Tuesday, 5 July 1988.
7   John F. Burns, "After 174 Years, 28 M.L.A.'s Return," *New York Times*, Friday, 1 July 1988.
8   Michael Clarkson, "Ceremony Ends Snake Hill Saga," *St. Catharines Standard*, July 2, 1988.
9   Ibid.
10   Ibid.

EPILOGUE

1   Fiona Gilchrist, "War of 1812 Graves Raise Interest," *Intercom*, 12, no. 6 (August 1988).
2   Pfeiffer, Susan and Ronald F. Williamson, eds. *Snake Hill: An Investigation of a Military Cemetery from the War of 1812* (Toronto: Dundurn Press, 1991).

INDEX

Abattis, 84, 92-93, 95
Age, 60, 133-35, 137
Ague, 103
American army. *See* United States Army
Amputation[s], 30, 64, 105, 109, 114, 116-17, 127, 131
Anatomy Act, 36-37
Anthropology, 22. *See also* Physical anthropologists
Archaeological assessment. *See* Archaeological survey
Archaeological consulting, 17, 23-24
Archaeological master plans, 18, 150
Archaeological Services Inc., 19-20, 23-24, 25, 30, 36, 41, 43, 66, 75, 76, 124, 139, 140, 142, 148
Archaeological survey (assessment), 16-17, 20, 22-23, 29, 37, 150
Archaeology, 17-18, 21-23, 25, 48, 124, 138-39
Archives, 80, 95, 132
Argyll and Sutherland Highlanders of Canada, 144
Arlington National Cemetery, 141
Arries, Kathleen O., 27-28
Arthritis, 82, 101
Artifacts, 23-24, 27, 29, 49-50, 64, 67, 76, 89, 90, 105-7, 112, 115, 118-20, 124-25, 127, 131-33, 140. *See also* Buttons
Artillery, 60-62, 65, 73, 84-86, 89-90, 92, 107-10, 125

Batavia, N.Y., 84
Bath, N.Y., 142
Bath National Cemetery, 145
Beattie, Howard and Valerie, 44, 147-48; property of, 44
Becker, General Quinn, 66, 67
Beirut, 140
Benn, Carl, 145
Bennett, Ross, 139
Biddle's Battery, 84
Bjarnason, Dan, 53
Black Rock, N.Y., 42, 84-85
British army, 29, 56-57, 59-61, 82, 85, 91-95, 92, 100, 110, 111, 116, 122
British North America, 26, 46
Brock, Maj.-Gen. Isaac, 46, 48, 80
Brown, Maj. Gen. Jacob, 56, 61-62, 65, 74, 79, 91, 98, 122, 125, 135, 141
Brown, Donald, 139
Buffalo Magazine, 153n.4, 154n.V,1
Buffalo News, 154n.IV,1, 154n.IV,2, 154n.V,3
Buffalo News Graphic, 153n.I,3
Buffalo, 18, 30, 42, 56-57, 66, 72, 79, 81, 91, 97, 101, 109, 110, 116, 117, 123-24, 141, 143
Burial 1, 29, 34-35, 112
Burial 2, 27-28
Burial 4, 73, 113, 127-28
Burial 5, 49, 63-64, 135
Burial 6, 134, 139

Burial 7, 69, 105-6, 134
Burial 10, 132, 133
Burial 12, 69, 105-7
Burial 13, 69, 105-7
Burial 15, 115
Burial 19, 73
Burial 20, 112
Burial 21, 112
Burial 23, 120
Burlington, Ont., 56, 61, 62
Burns, John F., 154n.V,7
Buttons, 25-26, 29, 34-35, 49-50, 67, 73, 78, 95, 105, 112, 119-20, 124-25, 127-30, 134, 139, 140

Canada, government of, 38, 39-40, 75
Canadian Armed Forces, 33, 66, 76, 123, 142
Canadian army. *See* Canadian Armed Forces
Canadian Conservation Institute, 49, 76
Canadian Parks Service, 38, 138
Candy, 54-55
Cemeteries Act, 17, 25, 30, 36-38, 149
Chartrand, René, 138
Chauncey, Commodore, 56, 61
Cheektowaga, N.Y., 141
Chippawa River, 58, 59, 122
Chippawa, Ont., 42, 58, 61, 62, 65, 122, 140; Battle of, 48, 59-61, 66, 80, 82, 116
Cholera, 101, 102
Clarkson, Michael, 153n.1, 154n.V,8, 154n.V,9, 154n.V,10
Class, 63, 136, 138
Clish, Andrew, 69, 72
Commonwealth War Graves Commission, 39
Community Facility Improvement Program, 75
Condren, Dave, 153n.I,3, 154n.V,3
Coroner's Act, 16, 30, 76
Cranial size, 77
Cybulski, Jerry, 77

Detroit, 46
Development, 17-18, 22-23, 37, 149-50
Diarrhoea, 101, 102
Diet, 97-98, 102, 113, 121, 127, 136-38
Disease, 97-98, 100-4, 115, 118, 121, 133
Douglass, Major, 32
Douglass's battery, 82, 85, 93, 96
Drugs, 103, 116
Drummond, Maj.-Gen. Gordon, 57, 58, 61, 62, 65, 91, 92
Dunlop, William, 116
Dunn, Vincent, 20, 38, 53, 147-48; property of (659 Lakeshore Road) 20, 25, 44, 48, 54, 72
Dysentry, 101, 102

Eden, N.Y., 141

Ellis, Stuart, 36-37
Environmental Assessment Act, 17, 22

Fenn, Julia, 49
Fenton, J., 154n.V,4
Fever, 101, 102, 103
First Nations, 16, 17, 19, 20, 22, 24-25, 29, 40, 46, 50, 57, 64, 127, 138
Fitzgerald, Marie, 36, 39
Flavelle, Dana, 153n.I,1
Fontaine's battery, 84
Fort Erie (fort), 15, 26, 29-31, 32, 41, 43-44, 48, 57, 65, 79, 82, 83, 85, 87, 88, 91, 103, 104, 108-9, 121, 123, 132, 134, 139, 140, 142, 143; siege of, 65, 82-85, 91, 97-98, 100-101, 114, 117, 118, 120-21, 123, 131, 132, 134, 135, 136; attack on, August 15, 1814, 29, 32, 91-95, 96, 98, 108, 135, 139, 145, 147-48
Fort Erie (town of), 15-18, 19-20, 24, 29, 31-32, 36-38, 40, 42, 48, 76, 78, 79, 123, 140, 141, 143, 147, 150, 153n.5
Fort Erie Guard, 143
Fort Erie Times Review, 154n.V,6
Fort George, 42, 56, 57, 61
Fort Niagara, 42, 56, 92
Fort Schlosser, 84
Fort York Guard, 143
Fox, William, 20, 36-37, 147
Fretz, Girve, 36, 39
Friendship Festival, 76, 123-24, 138, 140
Funding, 30, 36, 38-39, 147, 153n.5

Garner, Beverly, 69
George, David and Judy, 20, 38; house of, 20, 67; property of, 15, 25, 38, 44, 67, 71
Gilchrist, Fiona, 154n.E,1
Golden Horseshoe, 18
Gradall, 20, 25, 153n.5
Griffin, James, 143
Grinner. *See* Burial 2

Habsburg Jaw, 99-100
Haggerty, Ron, 36, 39
Hamilton Spectator, 75, 154n.III,1, 154n.V,5
Hasenauer, Heike, 154n.V,2
Hees, George, 143-44
Heritage, 17, 37, 40, 149
Hospital(s), military field, 27, 30, 79, 96, 104, 112, 112, 116, 117, 119-21, 123, 135
Hummel, Heinz, 19, 31, 36, 143, 144
Hygiene, 100-2, 114

Identification, 28, 54, 67, 124-35, 139
Intercom, 154n.E,1
Iroquois, 22, 24, 50, 57, 113
Isotopes, 63, 113; oxygen, 136-37; carbon/nitrogen, 34, 113, 127, 137-38

Jefferson, Thomas, 46

Johnson, Thomas M., 141
Journalists. *See* Media

King Tut, 21, 149
Kingston, Ont., 42, 56
Kloster, Donald, 139

Lake Erie, 16, 26, 30, 56
Lake Ontario, 18, 56, 91
Lakeshore Road, 15-18, 19, 40, 70
Landowners, 19, 20, 30, 36, 38, 44, 147-48
Lead, 63, 136, 137, 138
Lesions, skeletal, 86-88
Lewis, George, 16
Lewis, Patti, 153n.I,2
Llewellyn, Sgt. Lawrence (Jay), 49, 50
Lockport, N.Y., 54
London, Ont., 22-23
Lorenson, David, 15
Lundy's Lane 42, 62, 78, 85; Battle of, 48, 62, 65, 78, 82, 111

McCarthy, Robert J., 153n.I,3, 154n.V,3
MacDonald, Rob, 36, 72
McGill University, 22
MacLaughlin, Anne, 49, 51
McMaster University, 16, 79
Mann, Robert, 82, 98
Martin, Doug, 123
Matrons, hospital, 79, 104, 131
Matthews, Robert E., 110
Maxwell, Lois, 66, 68
Media, 15-16, 30, 31, 33, 36, 39, 51-54, 75, 109, 123, 141, 145, 147, 153-54
Medical system, 88, 96, 103-5, 108, 114-18, 121
Medical waste pits, 44, 67, 117, 139, 140
Micozzi, Marc, 77, 140
Militia (Canadian), 29, 46, 61, 143; Lincoln and Welland Regiment, 33, 36, 143, 145
Militia (U.S.), 46, 57, 60, 73, 81, 104, 107, 110, 123, 125, 129, 134, 135, 136, 139, 140
Ministry of Consumer and Commercial Relations – Cemeteries Branch, 17, 36, 149
Ministry of Culture and Communications, 39, 76, 147; Heritage Branch, 17, 20, 36
Ministry of Transportation, 23
Mix, Richard, 145
Moore-Jansen, Peer, 98
Murphy, Sean, 98
Museum of the History of Medicine, Academy of Medicine, 140

Napoleon(ic), 26, 46, 145
National Archives (U.S.), 80
National Museum of Civilization, 33, 77
National Geographic Society, 124
National Museum of Health and Medicine, 77, 82, 98, 108, 140
Native peoples. *See* First Nations

Neutral Indians, 16
New England, 137
New France, 41
New York State, 84, 137, 104, 110, 142, 145, 149
New York Times, 154n.V,7
Newton, Charlotte, 49, 51-52
Niagara Falls, 42, 58
Niagara Falls Review, 153n.I,2, 154n.II,2
Niagara frontier, 42, 48
Niagara Parks Commission, 38, 41
Niagara peninsula, 26, 29, 46, 56
Niagara Power Building, 140
Niagara Region, 36
Niagara Regional Police, 15
Niagara River, 16, 18, 31, 42, 56, 58, 62, 84, 91, 93, 139
Nicol, John, 15-16, 153n.3
Niles, Ambassador Thomas, 143-44
Noe, Adrianne, 108

Old Fort Erie. *See* Fort Erie (fort)
Old Guard, 143, 144, 145
Ontario Heritage Act, 37
Ontario, province of, 18, 19, 22-23, 137, 145, 149
Ontario, government of, 17, 19, 29-30, 33, 36-37, 40
Osteobiography, 77-79, 82, 86-87, 98, 101, 127, 134
Oswego, N.Y., 84
Ottawa, 31, 76, 77
Owen, David, 45, 154n.IV,3
Owsley, Doug, 72, 76, 82, 86, 98
Ox(en), 67, 70, 89-90, 91

Peace Bridge, 144, 146
Peace Bridge Authority, 140
Pennsylvania volunteers (militia), 57, 59, 81, 137, 140
Penton, B., 36
Peterson, Premier David, 75, 143
Pfeiffer, Susan, 77, 78, 135, 149, 154n.E,1
Physical anthropologists, 43, 49-50, 55, 72, 76, 79, 86, 95, 98, 101, 133, 135, 148
Planning, 16-20, 149-50
Planning Act, 16, 22, 37
Pneumonia, 101
Portage Road, 62
Porter, Brigadier General, 110
Porter's Brigade, 110, 123
Press conferences, 30-31, 52, 53, 123, 139
Property owners. *See* Landowners
Prosser, Lt.-Col. Daryl, 66, 67
Public Broadcasting Service (PBS), 51
Puking and purging, 103

Quartermaster(s), 78, 87-88, 91, 97
Queenston Heights, 42, 61, 98; Battle of, 48

Regular soldiers (British), 46, 57, 58, 61, 92
Regular soldiers (U.S.), 57, 59-60, 80, 97, 105, 125, 127, 129
Repatriation, 76, 139, 140-46, 147, 148

Reporters. *See* Media
Revolutionary War, 46, 100, 104, 140, 143
Rheumatism, 86, 101
Riall, Maj.-Gen. Phineas, 57-60, 62
Ripley, Brig. Gen. Eleazar, 57, 65
Robertson, Bruce, 36, 39
Rowan, Geoffrey, 153n.4, 154n.V,1
Royal Ontario Museum, 33, 49, 51, 75, 76, 79

Sacheli, Sarah, 154n.V,6
Sackets Harbor, 56, 84
Sackets Harbor Battlefield State Historic Site, 139
St. Lawrence River, 46
St. Catharines Standard, 15-16, 153n.1, 153n.2, 153n.3, 154n.V,8, 154n.V,9, 154n.V,10
Sandytown, 42, 104
Saunders, Shelly, 79
Schmorl's depressions, 86-87
Scott, Brig. Gen. Winfield Scott, 57, 59, 62, 65, 81-84, 101-2, 126
Scurvy, 98
Second War of Independence, 26. *See also* War of 1812
Secretary of the Army, 31
Secretary of war, 56
Seven Years' War, 41
Sex determination, 78-79
Shaughnessy, Tim, 32, 45
Sledzik, Paul, 82, 98
Smallpox, 101
Smithsonian Museum, 33, 43, 72, 77, 82, 98, 139
Snake Hill, 27-28, 32, 34, 36, 40-42, 47, 56, 60, 65, 72, 73, 77, 79, 80, 84, 85, 87, 91, 92, 95, 96, 97, 101, 104, 108, 109, 110, 111, 122, 123, 131, 132, 134, 136, 137, 139, 140, 141, 145, 146, 147, 148, 149, 150
Soldier, 154n.V,2
Sortie, 17 September 1814, 110-11, 122, 135
Stature, 53, 133, 135, 138
Steiss, Deborah, 31, 69
Stewart, Bill, 145
Stratford, Ont., 23
Street's Creek, 58, 59
Sumi, Craig, 154n.II,2
Summer Residents, Friendship Festival, 154n.IV,3
Surgeon(s), 102, 103, 104, 108, 111, 114, 116-17
Surgery, 34, 114. *See also* Amputation(s)
Swanson, Chris, 145
Swiss mercenaries, 92
Syphilis, 101

Tait, Eleanor, 154n.III,1, 154n.V,5
Teeth, 63, 98-100, 127, 134
Third U.S. Infantry. *See* Old Guard
Thomas, Stephen, 124, 139
Three Lads, 69, 105-7
Tohurst, Special Deputy William, 54-55
Toronto, 49, 56, 74, 139, 140. *See also* York
Toronto Historical Board, 139
Toronto Star, 153n.I,1

Toronto *Sun*, 66
Towson, Captain Nathan, 32, 85
Towson's battery, 32, 83, 84, 92, 95, 118, 135
Treaty of Ghent, 123, 124
Trepanning, 114
Trotter, Lt. Col. Robert, 31-36, 39, 45, 66, 67, 140, 142
Trowbridge, Amasa, 108
Typhus, 101, 102, 122

Uniform(s), 26, 34, 73, 95, 101-2, 105, 107, 112, 118-19, 125-27, 29
United States Armed Forces Institute of Pathology, 49, 66, 77, 82, 108, 139, 140
United States Army, 26, 28, 31, 33, 36, 39-40, 41, 44, 46, 60, 62, 65-66, 67, 76, 78, 80, 87-88, 92, 97, 99, 101, 103, 110, 123, 139, 143; supply system 1814, 88-91, 97, 103
U.S. Army Corps of Engineers, 32
United States Army Mortuary Affairs, 31
United States Army Total Army Personnel Agency, 31
United States Navy, 56, 91
University of Guelph, 77, 78
University of Tennesee, 98
University of Toronto, 77

University of Western Ontario, 21
Unknown Soldier, 141, 145
Upper Canada, 46
Usher's Creek. *See* Street's Creek

Veterans Affairs, 36-39, 143, 148, 149
Vietnam, 32, 140, 145
Vogel, Mike, 154n.IV,1, 154n.IV,2

War of 1812, 26, 29, 30, 33, 41, 45-46, 48, 56-62, 65-66, 68, 80, 87, 91-95, 99, 123, 141, 144, 145, 150
Washington, D.C., 31, 66, 76, 77, 79, 86, 140
Welland Tribune, 154n.II,1
White House, 80
Whitehorne, Lt. Col. Joseph, 31-32, 53, 79, 80-82, 86, 87, 91, 95, 97-98, 103, 108, 131, 134, 135, 136, 138, 140, 148
Wilder, Patrick, 139
Williamson, Ronald, 19-20, 21-4, 29-33, 36-38, 43, 45, 48-49, 53-55, 66-67, 68, 72, 75-76, 79, 82, 86, 98, 109, 134, 138-40, 144, 149, 153n.5, 154n.E,2
Williamsville, 104, 141
Wood, Major Michael, 31-32, 36, 131

York, 56, 57, 61, 74. *See also* Toronto

ONT___ HERITAGE FOU_____N

The

by Paul Litt, Ronald F. Williamson, and Joseph W.A. Whitehorne
Toronto: Dundurn Press, 1993